Cultu

CULTURE DEFEATS STRATEGY 2
Goonville, Texas

7 More Lessons on Leadership from a Texas High School Football Coach

Randy Jackson
Head Football Coach/Campus Coordinator
North Forney High School
Forney, Texas

What champions are saying about the 'Culture Defeats Strategy' series...

I'm a huge fan of Coach Jackson's 'Culture Defeats Strategy' and believe it belongs on the bookshelf of every head coach of any team sport. Culture Defeat Strategy 2 takes everything to the next level. Coach Jackson leaves no doubt about not only what a winning culture is but lays out exactly how to build it. If Culture Defeats Strategy belongs on every coaches' bookshelf, CDS2 belongs continuously open on every coach's desk. Thank you, Coach Jackson, for this masterpiece on how successful programs are really built.

Angus Reid
13 year CFL pro football player
2x Grey Cup Champion
Author of "Thank You Coach"

After advancing deep in the playoffs on multiple occasions but not quite getting over the hump, I began to look for ways to infuse fresh energy into our program that would inspire our kids to achieve more. Coach Jackson's book provided valuable insight into building a championship culture. There are many practical examples, laid out step by step, that we have used to dramatically change the culture of our program. Not only did we win a state championship, but more importantly, the impact our culture has made in developing our players into successful men will last a lifetime!

Travis Reeve
Athletic Director and Head Football Coach
Cuero High School, Cuero Texas
2018 4A-I State Champions

If you want to learn the details on how to instill a Championship Culture in your program or business, read Culture Defeats Strategy 2 by Randy Jackson! We have used many of his concepts as we are establishing the foundation of our program!

Jeff Jordan
Director of Player Personnel
SMU Football - #PonyUpDallas

Culture Defeats Strategy 2 - Goonville, Texas Pop. 11

Thank you, Coach Jackson, for sharing so many great lessons on how to develop outstanding culture in our program. We were able to immediately implement many of the concepts we read in the book and it made a huge impact in our program. We enjoyed tremendous success winning a Championship with a young team in 2017 and I was able to use these systems and see great success taking over at another school in 2018. There is no doubt in my mind that your strategies for developing a positive culture is the secret sauce for program success.

Jeff Steinberg
Head Football Coach
Beaumont High School, Cherry Valley, CA

Coach Randy Jackson does it again. He scores big on his second book, Culture Defeats Strategy 2. This book is an extension of his first one and is a must-read for all coaches and managers who are leading 'teams'. He is definitely a pioneer and at the fore-front of the next horizon in athletics – creating championship cultures.

Ben Blackmon
Head Football Coach
Spanish Fort High School, Spanish Fort, Alabama

Coach Jackson's stories and leadership process is relatable to all coaches. For teams who may have limited resources at the beginning phases of building a culture all the way to well-established championship programs, the CDS series is the go-to for creating an elite culture. At Greenup County High School, we not only read CDS but 'skyped' with Coach Jackson for 1 on 1 consulting. It was the best time we have invested in our program.

Scott Grizzle
Head Football Coach.
Greenup County High School, Greenup, Kentucky

When I started the culture journey three years ago, I knew exactly where to start...Randy Jackson. He provides proven methods and systems that will help any organization improve their culture. The tools and insights Randy shares in CDS 1 have been influential in helping me create a championship culture with our football and track programs at MRA. His methods will teach you how to act, communicate and treat other, just like I did with our wide receiver group the 'Air Raid Brigade'.

Culture Defeats Strategy 2 is a necessary read for any trailblazer looking to engage and inspire others to be ELITE. If you are looking to strengthen your team and accelerate results...invest in the CDS series.

John Weaver
Head Boys Track and Wide Receivers Coach
Madison-Ridgeland Academy, Madison, MS
2017 & 2015 State Track Champions
Culture Classroom Podcast Co-Host

Randy Jackson's cultural principles not only changed our football team, but even me as a coach. His culture ideas are the catalyst that allow us to give our players, teams, and program the absolute best opportunity to succeed.

Jeff Conaway
Athletic Director & Head Football Coach
Shiloh Christian School, Springdale, Arkansas
Home to 7-time 4A-Arkansas State Champions

I have had the opportunity to work for and be around thousands of coaches in my 23-year career and Coach Jackson is one of the very best I have ever seen at creating a standard that kids, parents and coaches believe in. He is passionate about creating a culture that teaches young people about values, humility, work ethic and caring for one another. He has a system and intentionally implements this every day where his program truly has an identity and reaches its full potential. I have been involved with Coach Jackson at three different schools and his kids are consistently respectful, hard-working, and enthusiastic. Coach Jackson's kids love to be in his program and they come out as better people because of it.

Geno Pierce CSCS, USAW-1Performance Course Inc.
www.performancecourse.com

Culture Defeats Strategy 2 - Goonville, Texas Pop. 11

Coach Jackson is an expert at turning around organizations and building cultures of excellence. Culture Defeats Strategy 2 is a masterclass in effective leadership. Coach Jackson applies his craft in and tells stories from the ultra-competitive world of Texas high school football where the margins between success and failure are often razor-thin. The lessons in this book are as applicable to leading businesses, professional service firms, churches, and families as they are to leading a football program. If you want to learn how to motivate and win the hearts and minds of your team, there is a blueprint in this book.

J. Clint Schumacher
High Stakes Trial Lawyer
Dallas, Texas

Having known Randy for a while and diving head first into his knowledge on culture, I feel like he is one of the best out there to learn from! Both his books, Culture Defeats Strategy and Culture Defeats Strategy 2, will be the difference in 2 to 3 games a year and make a difference in young people's lives forever! I'm ALL IN on Randy Jackson and The Culture Factory!

John Perry
Head Football Coach
Pearl High School, Pearl, Mississippi
Class 6A 16-0 State Champions

Randy Jackson is undoubtedly one of the 'kings of culture'. Randy and his Culture Defeats Strategy series has had a positive impact on me personally and our program. I have had the opportunity to spend some time with Coach Jackson and he is the 'real deal'. He has a unique gift to connect with people through his words, ideas and his stories.

Steve Jones
Head Football Coach
Kimberly High School, Kimberly, Wisconsin
150-6 Career record, 5-time State Champions

Culture Defeats Strategy 2

7 More Lessons on Leadership from a Texas High School Football Coach

©2019 by Randy A. Jackson

All rights reserved. No part of this book may be reproduced, stored in a retrieval system, or transmitted in any form or by any means (electronic, mechanical, photocopying, recording, or by any information retrieval system, or otherwise) without the prior express written consent of the author except for the inclusion of brief quotations in critical articles or a review.

Printed in the United States of America

Edited by: Donna Carroll and Cliff Gibson

Randy Jackson
Culture Defeats Strategy 2
7 More Lessons on Leadership from a Texas High School Football Coach

ISBN-13: 978-1654064914

ISBN-10: 1654064914

CONTENTS

PREFACE

ACKNOWLEDGMENTS

FOREWORD

AUTHOR'S NOTE

CHAPTER 1
A NEW FACTORY...............15

CHAPTER 2
LESSON #1 - EVERYTHING MATTERS...............37

CHAPTER 3
LESSON #2 - THE DAILY 'FIST-FIGHT'...............61

CHAPTER 4
LESSON #3 - HELP RAISE THEM UP...............94

CHAPTER 5
LESSON #4 - LEADERS EAT LAST...............116

CHAPTER 6
LESSON #5 - PRACTICE IS EVERYTHING...............145

CHAPTER 7
LESSON #6 - ELITE COACHING STAFFS...............181

CHAPTER 8
LESSON #7 - GOONVILLE, TEXAS POP. 11...............220

CHAPTER 9
'THE ANSWER IS YES' - S. CARROLL...............247

PREFACE

When I walked through the doors of North Forney High School, I immediately felt the palpable pains of a downtrodden, losing culture. The students and staff were unmanaged, unmotivated, and disengaged. The only pockets of success existed like small crowds desperately cowering under an umbrella in the middle of a downpour. As a leader of that organization, I knew it would be futile to start making changes in strategy or structuring or expectation, until I made significant changes in culture. However, I also understood that there were places within my organization that I alone could not fully impact. I understood that the culture of the entire organization was completely dependent on the question of whether or not I could change the aspects of our culture that impacted us the most. Everyone who knows anything about high school knows that football is an area of very high cultural impact on a school, in my opinion, the highest. This is why I knew that one of my first, and most important, missions was to find someone who was capable of partnering with me to rebuild the athletic culture of the North Forney Falcons. Once I committed to this mission and did my research, it did not take me long to commit to bringing Coach Randy Jackson to our campus as Head Football Coach and Campus Athletic Director.

Although I could not have foreseen what a major impact he would have in such a small-time period, I knew from the beginning that change would come. Coach Jackson makes change because he does not waste time opening umbrellas. He understands that, although it may be tougher at first, focusing on changing mindset and daily behaviors, is far more important than X's and O's. He

Culture Defeats Strategy 2 - Goonville, Texas Pop. 11

knows that everything matters because our smallest acts are a reflection of who we are at our deepest core, and if we are not winners at our deepest core, then we cannot ever reach our fullest winning potential. I am forever grateful to Coach Jackson for partnering with me to change the campus and community of North Forney High School. His work did not just turn a school around, it tore one down and rebuilt a new one in its place.

Read this book (and the original CDS), take notes, re-read it and implement as many techniques you can steal from Coach Jackson's journey through his career.

I will always be grateful for what he and his amazing staff did for the culture of North Forney High School and our community.

If you are committed to an 'everything matters' mindset, you can do the same for your organization.

Courtney Sharkey
Career and Technology Director
Richardson I.S.D., Richardson, Texas
(North Forney principal 2015-18

ACKNOWLEDGMENTS

It is with sincere and deep appreciation that I, Randy Jackson, acknowledge the support and guidance of the following people who helped make this book possible:

Thanks to Donna Carroll and Cliff Gibson for editing and encouraging me.

Thanks, Courtney Sharkey and Neal Weaver, for trusting and believing in me to help us change the culture at North Forney. I am so proud of the spirit that was created and honored to have been a small part of it. It's a work in progress but we've laid a foundation and aren't going to look back.

Thank you, Holly Abshire for helping more than any athletic trainer ever has in the spring and fall of 2017. You were an integral part of everything we did the first few months and beyond. I haven't ever worked with an athletic trainer who cares as much as you do.

Thank you, Megan Holder for being the greatest athletic secretary ever. You have all you done so much to help me personally and professionally, but even more important thank you for helping us 'raise them' by being a school mom to so many goons.

Thank you to the Goon Council Booster Club for always saying 'yes' and continuing to help us build the monster. Elite programs have elite booster clubs!

Thank you 'Original Goons' from the 2017 season. Players, parents and coaches will have lifetime memories of the birth of an identity of not only a football program but an entire community.

FORWARD

In January of 2016, I got on a flight from Redmond, Oregon to Dallas, Texas with the hope of being able to visit a few Texas High School programs while they were conducting their off-season program. Over the course of my career as a head coach, both wrestling and football, I have found that going outside of the area where I live to pick the brains of coaches who are doing what I want to do is the best professional development activity I have found.

During a Texas High School Football Chat on Twitter, a coach mentioned that for culture, visiting @coachjacksontpw was worth the trip. I direct messaged Coach Jackson asking if I could visit and he promptly responded. During my visit, we talked about culture, the daily struggle that a head coach must go through to be intentional both with himself as well as with his coaches and players. While I visited for half of a day, the 30 minutes we talked about being more to get more, and the importance of core values gave me enough to go home and get started working on building the culture I wanted within my own program.

Later that year, Randy's first book Culture Defeats Strategy was released and I was able to read it prior to the start of our season. I made notes and like all good coaches, borrowed liberally from the practical examples that Coach Jackson outlined in the book. We had already implemented our core values and I had sold to my coaches and players the importance of working daily on living those core values. We had the players recite our core values to get their helmet decals. Each coach was assigned a day for a leadership lesson prior to the start of practice. Our gear, posters, locker room and practice plans, all tied into our core values. The esprit de corps was high, we had a great preseason and the sky was the limit.

Culture Defeats Strategy 2 - Goonville, Texas Pop. 11

Then we started 0-3.

While sitting in our weekly coaches meeting on Sunday following the third straight loss to open the season, we had to confront the decision of whether we were to pivot or persevere. It was at that moment that we made the choice to double down on our core values and focus not on the outcomes of our games but on our vision, values and standards.

The next game we beat a play-off team 56-28 (they scored 21 in the 4th quarter after we had put the JV team in and went on to come within one play of winning the league title. Eventually, because of our poor start, we drew the 3rd seed in the state play-offs. We were able to defeat that team 35-27 and ultimately advanced into the state quarterfinals. The amazing thing about the victory over the third seed was that this was a team that beat us in Week 2.

I fully credit the resilience and continued improvement of our team over the course of the season to the culture lessons I learned from Randy. Most coaches implement their vision, values and standards and then go back to the way they've always coached, as if checking a box or two will proactively solve their problems. Randy's example and what he shared in Culture Defeats Strategy provided a road map and reinforcement for not only taking the first step but how to continue that work.

Read this book, take notes and then take action. The strategies and examples outlined within are proven to work and will help you improve both the outcomes and experience you have within your program.

Nathan Stanley
Athletic Director Lakeridge High School
Lakeridge, Oregon

AUTHOR'S NOTE

A couple of years ago, I took the plunge and 'put myself out there' by writing a book. This challenge was not an easy thing to do; you put yourself out there when you place your thoughts and experiences on paper. I didn't want to come across as arrogant in any way. My motivation was to hopefully sell 100 copies of Culture Defeats Strategy and have something for my grandkids if I ever have any to read one day. I also found out Amazon will print books, and you don't have to have your work approved to get it published. All right then, I'm in!

I love teaching and felt like I had learned a few things in the past couple of years that could help others build a championship culture. I wrote CDS to give others a clear way to incorporate core values into their program and used a few stories to help make it all stick.

CDS 2 - Goonville, Texas, Pop. 11, is the next edition in the Culture Factory series. This book will give you a first-hand account of how we turned North Forney (which we branded Goonville) into a winner the first year and ways you can make your program or organization elite in every way.

Thanks for allowing me to teach again with CDS2. I am honored you are reading it and hope you will get a few 'take homes' from it.

Remember, it's a 'daily fist-fight' to create an elite culture.

Let's GO!

CHAPTER 1
A NEW FACTORY

> **"CULTURE EATS STRATEGY FOR BREAKFAST."**
>
> **Peter Drucker**

February 27, 2017 - *"It won't stop coming up! It won't stop coming up,"* yelled Jordan Carroll, who was on his hands and knees away from the group of Falcon football players I was addressing. Jordan was one of the top returners from the previous season, a team leader and a future captain. This was my first official day at North Forney High School. We had just completed a not-so-tough offseason workout of 3 x 200-meter runs. The players were dead tired and fifteen of them didn't make it without getting sick. *Fifteen* threw up from running the equivalent of a little more than a warmup for most track teams.

We had given them plenty of rest between the runs so I was more than in a little bit of shock. This was the first step in the journey we were about to undertake together and we had to figure out a way to work them like they didn't think was possible, fascinate and inspire them, and teach them totally new offensive, defensive and kicking game schemes. Jason Bachtel, formerly the athletic director and head and football coach at Scurry-Rosser High School came to North Forney as the offensive coordinator and was with me from day one that spring. What a blessing, to say the least, to have Coach Bachtel help navigate the waters from the beginning. I will always be grateful for how he helped in the 'daily fist-fight' (more on this later) to flip the mindset of 100+ eager young men.

North Forney High School was the perfect storm for someone to come in and change the culture. There was talent; the administration was willing to make changes; the parents were eager and ready...the list goes on and on. It was time for the Falcons to emerge, and I was glad to be a part of it.

I always say, 'turning around a program is not for the faint of heart,' and North Forney was no exception. We had plenty of help, or it would not have happened.

Before we go too far down this road in CDS 2 — Goonville, Texas, Pop. 11, I need to give a disclaimer; this can be a stand-alone book, but it will not be as effective until you read the original Culture Defeats Strategy. It is a manifesto for how vital core values are to every program, a system to instill them, and many tools to be intentional with your culture. Phil Truax, athletic director of Lexington ISD in Nebraska, calls CDS a 'paint by numbers' book on how to build a culture in a program. CDS 2 will take core values and creating a championship culture to the next level with the systems we used at North Forney. Once you know the why and how of core values, you will be able to take the information in this book and help yourself, and your team thinks, talk, and act the same way.

Culture Defeats Strategy 2 - Goonville, Texas Pop. 11

In the first Culture Defeats Strategy, I laid out my career and my many stops to give the reader some insight into who I am why I felt led to write about culture. I won't bore everyone again with all of this, but in case you haven't read CDS, here's a little about me.

I am in my 30th year as a coach and educator in the state of Texas. I've been a head coach for 20 seasons and have a career win total of 161-82. My journey leading football programs began in 1999 in the small west Texas town of Paducah (115 in high school at the time and even lower now). After two successful seasons, my travels took me from Mason (200 in HS) to DeKalb (300 in HS) to Lone Oak (280) to Mesquite Poteet (1,800 in HS) to Plano East (6,000 in HS) to Grapevine (1,950 in HS) to finally North Forney... whew! (my fingers got tired typing this) I agree this list is too long, but I am wiser from the journey.

The most important lesson I have learned from all the moves is to be more careful before leaping to a new job. Our family moved because of distance from grandparents - I've been fired - I left because of broken promises and I've left because I wasn't a good fit with the administration. Every move was hard on my family, coaches' families, student-athletes, booster clubs, and admin. Some, not all, could have been avoided if I had done more research and slowed down a little. We just did a personality profile in FISD, and I am very high on 'aggressiveness' and very low on 'self-control,' so I am the poster child for needing to learn from others' mistakes. I wasn't a reader as a young coach, but I remember thinking, 'why isn't there a book or two from high school coaches about basic football and tips to move up in the profession?' There may have been, but if there was, I didn't know about them (pre-internet). I hope this book will help young leaders and veterans alike on their journey.

"A SLEEPING GIANT"

I had coached against NF when I was at Mesquite Poteet in 2012 but hadn't kept up with them. I always thought it was a "sleeping giant" type of place that was growing and had the athletes to win. In December 2016, the job was posted, but it didn't cross my mind to apply.

As with so many things in life, my timing and God's timing were not on the same time-line. I knew the odds of the job being open again in a couple of years were very slim, so I contacted a parent of one of my former players who had moved to NF, Carla Suits. I asked her if she thought the community and school district was hungry to make it happen. Craig Suits, the Suits' oldest son, was on our team back when I was at Poteet, but the family had moved to Forney, and their younger son, Colby, was the returning starting quarterback for the Falcons. I knew Carla would be able to tell me if NF had the same support we had at Poteet, so her opinion mattered to me. "Everyone is ready, Coach Jackson. We have all the pieces in place for this to be a good situation. The players, parents, and admin are all set to turn it around."

Carla's encouragement was enough for me to take the next step and reach out to the athletic director, Neal Weaver. Coach Weaver and I knew each other somewhat, but with my being on the other side of the Metroplex for the last four years, we had not crossed paths in a while. Neal is precisely the type of administrator I enjoy being

Culture Defeats Strategy 2 - Goonville, Texas Pop. 11

on 'his team.' He is relational, supportive with the tough issues, always ready to help, and has the highest of integrity.

The next thing I had to do (and I recommend to everyone who is looking at applying for a head job anywhere) is find out if the principal and I would get along. Courtney Sharkey was the principal and had been in the position for only a little over a year. For the Athletic coordinator/head football coach, the most important relationship you have is with your building principal. There is NO GRAY AREA here whatsoever. I have 'hoped for the best' on this and been disappointed a time or two in the past. This time I was going to be much more intentional to make sure she was committed to making the necessary changes. Ms. Sharkey was committed 100%.

"I know to change this entire school; we must find someone who will come alongside me and get the culture right in athletics. The culture you establish and the culture of the school go hand in hand," she told me when I interviewed her (the 2nd interview in the process). I was sold Courtney was not just telling me what I wanted to hear. One day when I retire, she will be on my 'Mount Rushmore' of favorite administrators in my career.

Change is extremely hard in any situation, and you must have a principal with the commitment and courage to help you make the changes. How do you know if your principal is willing to do this for the program to grow? You must ask for real change in the interview. A couple of great, no extra funding examples for me is the athletic period and teaching fields. Ask if they are willing to move the athletic period (if you are lucky enough to be in a state with one), ask if they are willing to work with you on teaching fields to help you hire quality teachers/coaches. If you don't get the right answers, DO NOT take the job and hope for the best like I have done a couple of times. There is no way to turn around a program without a commitment from your administration. Even if you have the talent to win, you will always be frustrated that the program could achieve more if you had the right systems in place.

OUR FIRST TEAM MEETING

Before I started at NF full time, I asked Courtney if I could have a team meeting with all the returning players in the auditorium so I could introduce myself and let them know what the program was going to stand for. I spent a lot of time on my presentation because I knew it would be an essential first impression.

I didn't just read a powerpoint about what they could expect moving forward but did my best to WIN THEM OVER that day. I knew it was vital they leave inspired after our time together. We discussed several aspects of what our program will be about and what they could expect from me and what I would expect of them.

- It will be a program they can't live without.

- We will be a leadership academy that happens to play football.

- They will earn everything they get every day.

-We will be driven by core values which they will help create.

Culture Defeats Strategy 2 - Goonville, Texas Pop. 11

-It will be the toughest thing they do in high school but the best thing also.

-Our program will become relevant in the area and the entire state of Texas.

-I will hire coaches who will help raise them up. Ones who would eventually 'lay in traffic' for the players if they had to.

It was a semi-formal setting in the auditorium with a few visitor's present. In addition to Courtney, assistant superintendent Rick Geer, Weaver, and Steven Carroll, our booster club president was all there in addition to a few others. People were excited to see the presentation and the vision for NF football. It was GO TIME for a new Falcon era.

Like everything, the meeting was good and bad. I brought lots of 'juice' during the presentation. I had done this a few times before and felt good about the message. I saw faces of excitement and hope. I told the freshmen not to worry because they had enough time to be made into OKG's (our kind of guys), but the seniors to be had to buy in quick if they wanted to leave a legacy.

CLARITY IS THE MOST IMPORTANT ASPECT OF EVERY MISSION. FIND WAYS TO MAKE SURE YOUR MESSAGE IS CLEAR AND ATTAINABLE

There were also a couple of times I couldn't believe how much talking was occurring by the players as I was presenting. Some of them had a hard time staying focused and respectful for the 60 minutes. On a couple of occasions, I had to look at a group of them and say, "if this is the best you can do with respect, we will not get along very well. 'The new north' will not be the program for you." As much as I wanted them to leave fired up and excited, I couldn't let them think this behavior was going to be ok. It was the first of many challenges this group would give us.

I love the 2017 Falcon football team, and I will praise them throughout this book but as a group, but they had a lot of issues we had to correct if we were going to get the most out of all the talent we had. When I arrived, most of them realized there were deep-seated behaviors that had to be addressed. They were not a true team but a group of individuals who would admit to selfishness, a lack of self-respect, and commitment. They wanted it to be fixed but didn't know how to do it and sure didn't know what it would take. Culture Defeats Strategy 2 will address how we intentionally changed the culture of the team, grew their identity, and in the process affected the entire school.

> *"Vison with action can change the world."*
>
> **Nelson Mandela**

IF YOU'RE WALKING YOU'RE WRONG

About a week after the introductory presentation to the team I began full time at North. Day one was something I will never forget. The male athletes had third-period for 'athletics' and when the bell rang Coach Bachtel, Coach Patton (another new coach who was coming to join the staff) and I were waiting in the hall for them to get dressed for workouts. We were excited to get going but if they were it was hard to tell. When they came through the doors leading to our athletic hallway they were committing the cardinal sin ... they were walking.

It was all I could do to keep it together but with experience comes wisdom. I knew they did not know any better. They were doing what they were used to doing. It would be the last day they walked to workout, because from then on Coach Bachtel and I stood in the hallway, blew our whistles and 'high-fived' them as they ran to get their workout gear on. We made it a high energy, 'juiceful' experience for them and let them know it was the best part of our day seeing them.

We inherited an outstanding group of seniors at NF who were hungry to change the perception and history of the program but as all of you know talent is never enough. My definition of culture is; how your team thinks, how your team speaks and how your team acts. We had work to do to get them on the same page with all three.

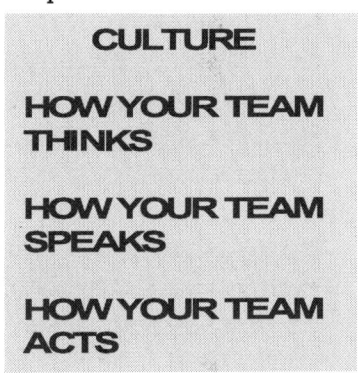

CULTURE

HOW YOUR TEAM THINKS

HOW YOUR TEAM SPEAKS

HOW YOUR TEAM ACTS

When I take over a new program I always take a 'lay of the land' and assess areas that have to addressed first. It didn't take long to realize the areas we had to fix and fix quickly. Work ethic (the first day on the track was an eye-opener), the concept of TEAM, and discipline was first on my agenda.

It is hard to put into words all the changes we made the first few months. Just the first month could be a book itself but I will attempt to do my best in the first couple of chapters to explain how we attacked with intentionality to mold them into the 'goons' they eventually became.

"IT'S NOT YOUR FAULT TODAY BUT IT WILL BE SOON"

A young farmer was covered in sweat as he paddled his boat up the river. He was going upstream to deliver his produce to the village. It was a hot day, and he wanted to make his delivery and get home before dark. As he looked ahead, he spied another vessel, heading rapidly downstream toward his boat. He rowed furiously to get out of the way, but it didn't seem to help.
He shouted, "Change direction! You are going to hit me," but the boat did not move and kept coming right at him. The vessel hit his boat with a violent thud. The farmer shouted, "You idiot! How could you manage to hit my boat in the middle of this wide river?"

As he glared into the boat, seeking out the individual responsible for the accident, he realized no one was there. He had been screaming at an empty boat that had broken free of its moorings and was floating downstream with the current.

This story is exactly the way many organizations operate. They hope for the best and no one is really driving the boat. In sports, coaches will know the technique, scheme, have a practice plan, etc. but that is not what really drives the boat.

When you take over a new program keep in mind everyone does what they have been conditioned to do. We are all creatures of habit and will act how we are allowed. Just like with the guys walking to athletics the first day because they were conditioned to walk we must make it crystal clear every expectation we have.

With culture, you will get what you deliberately create. If you just 'let it happen' no one will be driving the boat and the years you have more talent than others you will win a lot of games. During the seasons your talent drops you will not be successful. To build a championship culture, you must win a little each day. It is like investing in the stock market. Wall Street rewards the long-term investor with small gains over time. You can't invest one day, pull your money out and then invest again a week later. Investors who stay the course are rewarded for their commitment. This is exactly how growing and creating a culture happens.

One of the reasons the original Culture Defeats Strategy was so successful was because it laid out *systems* the reader could follow and wasn't a book of generalities. This is what CDS 2 will do also. My hope is you will be able to take this book and use several systems to either take over a new program or change the one you have now.

GROWING PAINS OF NEW EXPECTATIONS

It is important to get your new group to invest more than they are used to. Our athletic period was from 10:30-11:20 but this was not nearly enough time to meet with them each day, begin the 'brain washing' process and establish the new work ethic standard. Like I always do in this situation, I asked them to come in before school and voluntarily lift weights. The first day we had 30+ in

Culture Defeats Strategy 2 - Goonville, Texas Pop. 11

the weight room and the guys were excited about the turnout. Like most coaches, I was happy with the turnout but disappointed all of our better players were not in attendance. I knew we wouldn't get them all there because some rode the bus to school but we were missing some key rising seniors who were starters the year before. Each day our numbers improved for before school workouts but only because we wouldn't take no for an answer.

Our attendance for athletics during the day was also disappointing in the beginning.

"My parents are divorced and we stayed with our mom last night who lives over thirty minutes away."
"I didn't have a ride."
"My alarm clock didn't go off."

"I had a dentist appointment."

Coaches, stop me if you've ever heard any of these before. After the initial excitement of the new leadership and program the reality set in that the expectations were dramatically different.

"We can make this an evolution or a revolution. I am not a patient man so I vote for revolution," I told them within the first couple of days. "The recipe is proven but we can't do it for you. I have seen it both ways - one where the seniors were sick of losing and would eat sand if I asked them to and one where they thought they were sick of it but when it came time to do the work they were just fine with status quo. If you just WANT to turn it around we won't. If you really NEED to turn it around and can't stand it anymore we can get it done this year. The new way we are doing things is the only way for a

Culture Defeats Strategy 2 - Goonville, Texas Pop. 11

revolution. If you want to do it your way then we will change the culture after the season when you are no longer around." You must be real with your seniors from Day 1. No matter how good your underclassmen are, the seniors you inherit will almost always determine how the first year goes.

Most coaches get through season one and wait for the offseason to make major behavior changes but that is not how I live. I'm always in a hurry but more importantly, it is not doing the seniors justice to take this approach. High school is a small window for them and we were going to do our best to allow them to be heroes in their senior year story.

After one week of workouts I decided to have a senior-only meeting before school. We do this periodically to 'assess, address, and progress.' Basically, we go over how things are going. I tell them what I am seeing both bad and good and allow them to talk. I especially want to get a sense of how the team is taking to the new ways we are doing things. This approach has served me well over the years. High school students, in general, want to be heard, they want to share their dreams and be a part of the process.

Tim Krause, head coach at Bishop Kenny High School in Florida was scheduled to visit that day so I told him to come early and sit in on the meeting. Coach Krause sat in the back while Coach Bachtel and I were in the front of our team meeting room in our athletic facility. At 7:55, I started to get a little concerned because we were missing several athletes.

At 8:00, I shut the door and counted — we had 19 of our 33 seniors present. I have seen a lot of things over the

Culture Defeats Strategy 2 - Goonville, Texas Pop. 11

years so it is hard to shock me but I was a somewhat amazed, not very happy and more than a little bit embarrassed with a coach whom I respected, visiting. A few minutes later a couple more came in late (I normally wouldn't allow them in but I made an exception so they could hear my displeasure).

That night we had our first parent meeting and my mission was the same as my first meeting with the players – energize, inform and launch our identity. I laid out the vision, our systems, what we needed from the parents and a great booster club. I covered everything I could think of to inspire them and let them feel my passion for creating a new culture. I even had a parent of an ex-Grapevine player, Greg Rice, speak to them about what to expect and what it took to build up the program there. "Be ready for Coach Jackson to work your son harder than he's ever been worked, but he will be loved on just as hard," Greg said.

The most important thing we discussed was what happened in the morning with the senior meeting. "Unless we get this fixed nothing else matters. Until they can be counted on, until we can trust them it will not change. Be ready for them to come home and tell you it was a hard day. NF football will be a leadership academy that happens to play football. We will pour into them every day and help you raise them but we will not have a program that allows them to show up when they want to or be late without major consequences. Accountability will be very high and your son may or may not enjoy it. If he is not used to a high degree of accountability it will be a major change for him. The ones who can't live without it are going to love the changes. The ones who can probably won't make it." I wasn't sure how they would take it but it had to be said.

A few started clapping, the rest joined in and then stood up and gave us a standing ovation! We were on our way now.

THE STANDARD MUST BE THE STANDARD

Did we lose a few who could live without it the first few months? We did. I do believe participation numbers are important and I am all for as many as we can get to play but not at the expense of lowering our standards. When I was a young boy I remember dunking on an 8-foot goal and feeling pretty good about myself. There are no 8-foot goals on Friday nights in Texas high school football or in any other state or any other sport. High-five them, tell them you love them, make sure they feel your heart and passion but do not under any circumstances lower the standard to keep a few who live in the 'land of the uncommitted.'

What about the player we *must have*? What about the guy who is our fastest running back or the leading tackler? When you are the leader your team is watching closely to see if you are what you say you are. Don't get me wrong, we are not looking to dismiss players. We want to mentor them and grow them into men of character but when you first take over a program that needs an overhaul you cannot, under any circumstances, flinch. It can be a revolution but only if you change the mindset and behaviors. Almost all of them will want the program to change but some will not want to change their behaviors and habits.

For a jet plane to get into cruising altitude it uses the majority of its energy to get off the ground. Once it's stable and flying, it does not require the same amount of fuel to maintain. This is how it is when you first take over a program. Make it clear, make it firm, and make sure they understand you are helping to raise them. By all means, hold them accountable to the Nth degree every day. Until your staff commits to this, a big change cannot occur.

TOUCH THE LINE BUT DON'T BE ON IT

Discipline is one of our core values and always will be. Teams in every sport who win consistently do it with discipline. After a few weeks, I decided to see if we could all stand at attention, feet together and toes precisely on the edge of one the yard lines on the field. I haven't ever asked a team to do this before but thought it would prove a point. This sounds so simple but it was not easy to get them all to do this especially after we got them tired. The coaches and I would 'inspect' them and one foot wouldn't in contact with the other or there would be a little 'green' (the field) between their toes and the yard line. Again, I have been doing this for almost thirty years and it was amazing to me we couldn't get this simple assignment done. They would be exhausted  and I would yell, "get on the line in Falcon position." They would stretch all the way across the field and one or two would be off just a little. "We still can't get right! Everyone down and bear crawl to the goal line!" They would bear crawl and then it all started over again. The

Culture Defeats Strategy 2 - Goonville, Texas Pop. 11

Friday before spring break they were mentally checked out and already on vacation. Coach Bachtel and I had been there about three weeks and wanted to send a message so we ran more than usual. Fewer players were getting sick but it was a tough workout. One of our guys who had come from basketball and did not have quite as much time to get acclimated to the new standard was struggling to get 'on the line but not touch it'. He was a returning starter and a good player but he was used to having it his way a little (or maybe a lot). When we inspected the team in Falcon position he was not getting it done and we kept bear-crawling them.

> *"If your team isn't doing what you need them to do, you first have to look at yourself. You have to figure out a way to better communicate it to them in terms that are simple, clear and concise."*
>
> **Jocko Willink, Author**
> **Extreme Ownership**

From experience, I could tell he was seeing if we would eventually let it go. He and I were getting in a 'urinating contest' and this was going to be one of those moments where he and the rest of the team was going to find out if I was going to be a man of my words, or let my standard slide to avoid a confrontation with a good player. He found out and more importantly the team did that the standard was going to be he standard. I got loud in my displeasure and we got pretty close to a confrontation... It was one of those unforgettable teachable moments. We wouldn't see them for over a week and they left thinking, "He isn't going to bend for the prima donnas." I'm sure some were grateful and some knew they were going to have to change.

Culture Defeats Strategy 2 - Goonville, Texas Pop. 11

There are two major points from this 'touch the line' demand we gave them and the confrontation. Scouts honor, I am not exaggerating but it took the better part of a month to accomplish this small act of discipline. Just like the meeting where so many were absent, I knew the revolution wouldn't happen until we had some self-discipline.

Under any circumstances do not bend for the one player (or more) that you think you can't live without. All of them are important but none are worth having two standards. My greatest fear is 90% of our team thinks we are not doing what we say we will do and that as a coaching staff we are frauds. This does not mean we don't try very hard to save everyone. We do all we can to work with them, counsel, pick them up, whatever we can do other than lower the standard for them. 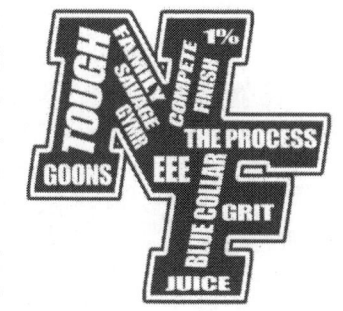 If we would have had to lower the expectation, bend, look the other way to keep someone who can live without being in the program then everything I said the first day I met them in the auditorium would have been invalid. There were plenty of days where a few guys didn't want to run down the hall to athletics. If we would have looked the other way then what else would they want to get away with? Everything hard.

WHAT IS BUILT FAST IS NOT BUILT TO LAST

I used Chapter 1 to give you an idea of where we started. Like most good stories, there will be a happy ending. In

Chapter 8, you will see the growth and attitude change of our 'goons' and how far we grew as a team. The biggest take home from the first few weeks I want you to get is address - access, address - access and address some more. Give them hope with your vision you share daily and do it with juice and passion they can feel. Each situation is different so decide what the team you are inheriting needs and attack it relentlessly. Do not sacrifice the foundation you must set in the beginning to keep a few who can live without it. The 90% who are doing everything right are counting on you.

THE VISION OF GOONVILLE

Walt Disney had a vision in the 1950's for a place much more than an amusement park with the typical midway games and typical rides for kids. He wanted a magical place unlike any other for the entire family to enjoy.

Construction began in 1954 with a goal of it being completed by July of 1955. In fact, to add stress to the situation, Mr. Disney told a television audience on his own show about the park and that it would open in 11 months.

Mr. Disney was heavily involved in the project. He was on site almost daily going over blueprints and deciding day-to-day decisions.

The most inconvenient, non-negotiable for Disney was the building of Cinderella's Castle before anything else. The contractors begged him to allow them to start on other projects first. Building the castle from the start would not only increase the overall cost of Disneyland but more importantly would slow down the project that was already going to be a race against time to make the deadline.

Disney did not budge. He stood his ground and the castle was built first. Why was this so important to him? He wanted all to see his vision. The castle was amazing and would be the central inspiration of the entire park. Disney wanted all who came to see the progress that his vision was going to produce and how 'one-of-a-kind' the park was going to be.

All the tough times we had in the first few months at NF was necessary to get our 'park' built. Every day myself and our staff had to share the vision of what it could become, and what it must become quickly for our talented group of rising seniors to be a part of it. I told this story of Cinderella's Castle at our football banquet and thanked everyone for believing in the vision. The next few chapters is how we went from not being able to 'touch the line but not be on it' to a relevant football program. Not only did the program change but a school and community did as well.

CHAPTER 1 REVIEW
LAYING THE FOUNDATION

- The job is open for a reason. Expect challenges as you establish the new standard.

- Have a semi-formal team meeting to lay out your vision and the systems you will use to achieve it.

- Bring the juice! Although we were working them harder than they were used to, we were also high-fiving them through it.

- Get the lay of land and handle each new place a little different. Some places need a cheerleader and some need a drill sergeant.

- Remember, in the beginning it's not their fault ... yet.

- Everyone needs each other to build a new culture. Include them in the process.

- Have patience but don't sacrifice the standard for the small percentage who are toe-dipping with the changes.

- As they are going through the pain of change remind them often to not focus on what they are 'going thru, but what they are going to.

CHAPTER 2
LESSON #1 – EVERYTHING MATTERS

> *"The devil is in the details, and everything we do in the military is a detail."*
> **Hyman Rickover**

"*For the want of a nail, the shoe was lost,
For the want of a shoe, the horse was lost,
For the want of a horse, the rider was lost,
For the want of a rider, the battle was lost,
For the want of a battle, the kingdom was lost,
And all for the want of a horseshoe nail.*"
— Benjamin Franklin

This version of "The Horseshoe Nails" by Benjamin Franklin is probably the most well-known in the U.S. but the earliest use of 'the nail analogy' is found in the work of Freidank, an early 13th-century poet from what is now Germany.

Freidank wrote:
*The wise tell us that a nail keeps a shoe,
A shoe keeps a horse,
A horse keeps a knight,
A knight who can fight keeps a castle.*

This poem resonates with me because it is a warning about the importance of little things. EVERYTHING MATTERS because everything little thing counts when you are changing a culture. 'For the Want of a Nail' is also powerful because it is told in hindsight. People who do not pay attention to detail oftentimes are the ones who look back on a situation and think, 'if only we would have nipped that in the bud' or 'I should have known that behavior was going to get worse.'

Everything matters could be an entire book for me. I learned from great coaches as a player and as an assistant that 'attention to detail' is an edge. In this chapter, we will look at how 'Everything Matters' has been emphasized by some legendary coaches and how we stress it every day at North Forney.

John Wooden took time in the first practice of the year (every year) to teach his Bruins the correct way to put on their socks to avoid blisters. Claudia Luther's article from UCLA Today in 2010 tells the reasoning of this attention to detail from Coach Wooden himself. He was speaking at a cancer benefit and used a 12-year old cancer survivor, Robert, to help him demonstrate.

Coach Wooden came out on stage holding a box with athletic shoes and socks. There was much good-natured laughter as Wooden gave Robert the socks-and-shoes instructions.

"You know, basketball is a game that's played on a hardwood floor," Wooden said. "And to be good, you have to change your direction, change your pace. That's hard on your feet. Your feet are very important. And if you don't have every wrinkle out of your sock ... "

The coach then took a black athletic sock and started to put it on Robert's foot, asking the boy to complete the task. Wooden: "Now pull it up in the back, pull it up real good, real strong. Now run your hand around the little toe area ... make sure there are no wrinkles and

Culture Defeats Strategy 2 - Goonville, Texas Pop. 11

then pull it back up. Check the heel area. We don't want any sign of a wrinkle about it ... The wrinkle will be sure you get blisters, and those blisters are going to make you lose playing time, and if you're good enough, your loss of playing time might get the coach fired."

To audience laughter, Wooden pulled out an athletic shoe.

"Now put it in wide, now pull it up," he told Robert. "Now don't grab these lines up here, go down, eyelet by eyelet ... each one, that's it. Now pull it in there ... Tie it like this... "The coach teased Robert gently as he explained why this was so important.

"There's always a danger of becoming untied when you are playing," he said. "If they become untied, I may have to take you out of the game — practice, I may have to take you out. Miss practice, you're going to miss playing time and not only that, it will irritate me a little too."

> **FOCUSING ON THE LITTLE THINGS IS A MUST TO CHANGE THE CULTURE. DEMAND THINGS TO SEE WHO WILL COMPLY AND WHO WON'T. FIND WAYS TO SEE WHO YOU CAN COUNT ON THRU REQUIRING ATTENTION TO DETAIL IN**

The coach talked Robert through double-tying his shoelaces so they wouldn't come undone. Then he talked him through taking the shoes off by untying the strings, eyelet by eyelet.

"You gonna remember that?" Wooden asked Robert. "I hope you never get any blisters."

@CoachJacksonTPW   #culturematters

I have been guilty of going too fast (I do love repetitions) and not making sure everyone is on the same page with a scheme (O, D, or kicking game) but when it comes to discipline not much gets past me. I've had more than one assistant tell me, "I don't think about checking for earrings," or "I got busy and didn't notice my position player was wearing the wrong undershirt" (insert about anything here). I still don't understand when everyone doesn't see everything. It must be a priority. Everyone is different and I'm sure many of you reading this do not worry about what undershirt your guys wear in a game but for me, it represents much more than a shirt. If you can't get your guys to wear the same thing then you are getting them to think, speak and act the same either.

> **"THE SECRET TO SUCCESS IS FOUND IN OUR DAILY AGENDA. WHATEVER YOU INVEST IN COMPOUNDS OVER TIME LIKE INTEREST."**
> Tag Short

100% is EASY, BUT 99% IS TOUGH

In the spring of 2018, I began to allow custom mouthpieces to be worn because I honestly got tired of fighting the few who wore them. While I don't think it's a major deal and not a distraction, during a staff meeting at the end of spring ball one of our coaches told me it allowed some gray area. What a great point, if you are going to say, "only wear what we give you," then that is what it needs to be. When you pick and choose what is allowed and what isn't then the clarity of the mission is lost.

Culture Defeats Strategy 2 - Goonville, Texas Pop. 11

Can there be compromise? Yes. We did eventually give a little on the mouthpieces. The fall of 2018, after meeting with our leadership council, we allowed custom mouthpieces as long as they were of school colors: blue, black, silver.

I laid out the culture we inherited and some of the issues we had to address in Chapter 1. We had lots of talent and guys that were tired of losing but none of that would matter if we didn't get them to buy into what we are were now selling.

What did we need to focus on the most to get them going in our direction? The little things had to be addressed daily. Nothing could be viewed as minor because it's all major when you're finding who can live without it and who can't.

What do discipline and acting right in the classroom have to do with tucking their shirt in during workouts? EVERYTHING. Everything you ask them to do is important. The key to core values is emphasizing them daily, and the key to attention to detail is demanding 100% every training session. We have the greatest military in the world because attention to detail is enforced one day and not the next. None of us would want to find out who we can count on after we're assigned to be in a foxhole with them. I will always do my best to determine who is 'all in' before we go to battle with them.

Back to 'For the Want of a Nail.' The battle that was lost was the Battle of Bosworth in 1485. King Richard III (the last English king killed in battle) was left stranded and horseless. He was defeated and ultimately killed, all because of a faulty horseshoe nail. William Shakespeare

@CoachJacksonTPW   #culturematters

Culture Defeats Strategy 2 - Goonville, Texas Pop. 11

writes in his epic play "Richard III," it was alleged he was thrown from his horse in battle because the blacksmith put one too few nails into the horse's shoe.

A PENNY IN THE FUSE BOX AND THE COLOR OF THE CARPET

'Back in the day,' homes had fuse boxes instead of the circuit breaker panels we have now. When a fuse burned out, it was protecting the house from the risk of a fire because each circuit was designed for a certain amount of current. The problem with this system was higher current created more heat and more heat could start a fire. So, they put fuses in that were designed to burn out before the wire would get hot enough to be dangerous.

One of my favorite phrases is everything is 'good and bad', and this is certainly the case because an immediate solution for a burned-out fuse was to put a penny in its place until the owner could go to the hardware store and replace it with an actual fuse. The problem was all too often people would forget they put the penny in the fuse box and leave it long term instead of replacing it quickly by installing a correct fuse. Back then, pennies were made of actual copper, and they would keep the 'juice' flowing at all times. When an overloaded circuit became overheated, there was nothing to stop the heat from continuing to rise and eventually start a fire. An untold

@CoachJacksonTPW   #culturematters

number of house fires were started before modern circuit panels replaced them.

Many times, coaches think something is not that big of a deal, and either doesn't want to deal with it or believe it will go away. We did not stick pennies in the fuse box at North. I read this analogy a few months ago in an article about the fall of Enron. The books were 'cooked' years before the public knew about the accounting issues. They kept finding ways to put Band-Aids on the problems, and eventually, it caught up to them. We do not win every game just like everyone reading this book does not, but everyone can do the extra, go to the proverbial hardware store, and address issues head-on before they become a crisis we could have avoided.

I had a pastor once tell me that churches split all over the world because church members do not agree on minor things that should not matter, like the color of the carpet. He used the analogy of a closed fist and an open hand on things churches should be focused on. The color of the carpet is an open hand item. Not that you can't have an opinion but certainly not a big enough deal to cause a rift. If the music minister is wearing jeans or a suit is (for me) an open hand issue. Jesus Christ being the son of God and dying for our sins, is a closed-fisted belief that all members of our church should agree on. There can't be a gray area on this for a Christian-based church.

What leaders of any organization have to do is determine what open hand or close-fisted for them is. As you can gather, for me, most things are closed-fisted in our program, especially anything that relates to discipline. Our creed is our core values defined, and we will live them daily. All we have to ask ourselves is 'does this represent our values or are we sticking a penny in a fuse box and letting something slide that will bite us

> **"If anything matters then everything matters."**
> **William Young**

WAYS WE LIVE 'EVERYTHING MATTERS' AT NORTH

You will get what you emphasize on a daily basis from your team. Daily may not be a strong enough description. I am continually going to fight the good fight to not stick a penny in a fuse box when it comes to discipline and attention to detail. I polled our players and coaches while writing this chapter of what they believe are 'everything matters' standards for us and things we demand constantly. There were lots of great answers of things we stress, like touching the line but not on it described in Chapter 1 but here are what they responded as closed-fist beliefs we use daily that help us achieve our culture of discipline and everything matters.

Finish through the line – I have an out of body experience when someone does not finish a drill at full speed. If I could only choose one thing on this list it would be *'finish.'* As coaches, we must set up our drills so there is a finish line and not some gray area of when an athlete can stop performing. A finish line is a physical line on a field or a cone. A whistle can also be a definitive end to an activity. I've seen tackling drills where a defender will execute the technique and then stop when he feels he has gone far enough. This is

Culture Defeats Strategy 2 - Goonville, Texas Pop. 11

something I stress to all my new coaches — when we tackle, they are to run their feet until they hear a whistle! Coaches must stand where they can see the finish line. The beginning of the drill is important but not nearly as much as the finish. We make sure we don't stand where they start and focus only there. Stand in the middle or towards the back of the drill and make sure you can see the burst through the line. If you allow an athlete to slow down before the finish, you're engraining in him/her a bad habit that will get you beat. When we do agility drills at North Forney, I'm prowling around looking at one thing - *FINISH*. On the rare occasion 'finish' doesn't happen to our standard, it will be addressed every time.

Red shirt system - In the first Culture Defeats Strategy I described our '?' shirt system and how we have our guys earn their way into the Elite locker room in the offseason. This past year, we added another shirt to our system - the red shirt for guys who have any type of discipline issue in the classroom. If any coach hears from a teacher that 'Johnny' needs to improve his attitude, he is given a 3x red shirt (doesn't matter how small he is because we want him to not enjoy wearing the shirt) and will wear it until the teacher tells us things have improved. We also have a count up clock we reset every time an athlete has to 'wear red.' What you measure you can improve. The clock is where we have our leadership academy/team meetings so all can see us take it back to zero and start the count up again. This off-season we will implement a reward, probably some type of food for the team, every time the clock hits 30 days without a red shirt issue.

The 'Pit of Misery' - in addition to our system of wearing a red shirt to make our guys feel mentally uncomfortable we ensure they are also physically uncomfortable when they have a discipline issue with a teacher or administrator, late to workout (we are a morning practice team) or have an unexcused absence. The 'price of irresponsibility' has to be paid and we collect every day. I will always have a coach who will take care of our discipline issues in the same place and at the same time. Our assistant coaches help make sure those on the list go to the pit. I will also discuss who is 'on the list' in front of the team during our daily Leadership Academy team meetings (we will discuss in detail in Chapter 3). I do not mandate the exact ways for our 'tough love' coach to enforce our standard in the pit. I just tell him to make sure it is safe, but uncomfortable. Some of the things we have done in the past are plate pushes (45 lb. plate pushed on the turf with both hands), lunges with a plate overhead, and bear-crawls, etc. I'm sure most of you understand the types of drills I'm referring to. We attempt to use activities that will benefit our guys in some way by adding strength or endurance. We used to jog a mile for an unexcused absence but we decided this only trains slow twitch muscle fibers so we no longer have them run for distance as a punishment.

Spin the Wheel - In 2019 we implemented a discipline wheel (think carnival type wheel) with different punishments. When a player is late, a teacher is not happy with him, etc. he will 'spin the wheel' before practice.

Hard Yards – this was given to us also in 2019 and it has been a great addition to our gauntlet of love tough. Players have 4 minutes to: log roll 100 yards, bear crawl 100 yards, back pedal 100 yards, forward roll 100 yards. My favorite aspect of hard yards is time is a factor. If they stop and rest more than our coach deems necessary they start over and begin again. Hard yards during our team warm up time which also takes right at four minutes.

Fist-to-Chin - University of Minnesota head coach PJ Fleck uses the phrase, "the ball is the program." He uses this stat to back it up; since 1950, 78% of all college and professional football games have been won by the team who is +1 or more in the turnover ratio. In any sport, more games are lost than won. We are going to do everything we can to take care of the ball. The term we used to use was, 'high and tight,' referring to the position of the football when we carry it. Now we use 'fist to chin.' This is a more concrete term with no gray area. We are always striving for clarity and 'fist to chin' achieves it. How often do we remind our guys to be 'fist to chin?' All The Time. Every time a receiver catches a ball and is jogging back to get in line he must be 'fist to chin.' We don't allow them to throw the ball back but they must jog it back with correct ball position and hand it to the coach or injured player who is snapping the ball. Now the drill is not only teaching our guys how to run the route but reinforcing how to protect it after the catch.

'Count On Me' Priorities and what constitutes an excused or unexcused absence - I learned this system from my good friend Rick Jones of Greenwood, Arkansas. Rick has won multiple state championships in his career and has been named National Coach of the Year by the AFCA, so when I get a chance to learn from him, I listen intently. One of the best systems Rick has

Culture Defeats Strategy 2 - Goonville, Texas Pop. 11

taught me is his 'Priorities' system for absences. If one of our players is not present, it certainly matters. For years I thought I had a pretty good way to communicate the difference in excused and unexcused, but I have been using this for a couple of years and it has taken the clarity of this to another level.

'Count On Me' Priorities in Goonville, Texas

1. God / Church

2. Family

3. North Forney Extra-curricular

4. Football

----

5. Everything else

Our athletes and parents know exactly what will be excused and what won't.

Miss for church activity? Priority #1 - *excused*
Miss for a dentist appointment? Priority #5- *unexcused*

Miss to participate in our school One-Act play?

Priority #3 - *excused*

Miss to go back-to-school clothes shopping? Priority #5- *unexcused*

*Before any workout where an athlete is going to be absent, excused or unexcused, **he** must text or call his position coach before it begins. It is not ok for a parent to reach out three hours after we are finished to let us know her son has a fever and wasn't able to join us. I tell our guys if they aren't present when we begin, I worry something might have happened to them on the way to practice, and I don't like to worry. Hopefully the 'hard yards' or the 'pit' will help them remember to let us know where they are.

Go on the Whistle – sometimes we will get our guys tired and not only have them stand where they are 'touching the line but not on it,' but also make them listen to certain commands to start the drill. My favorite and easiest version of this is just "go on the whistle." The drill begins with their hand behind the line (you must make sure because everything matters) and go when they hear a whistle. Simple, right? It's much tougher than it sounds. They are already tired, like they will be in the fourth quarter, they are wanting to compete and must resist the urge to go on the command they have heard since they were old enough to comprehend language – the word GO. Coaches, try this with your team and see if they can resist the 'go' command. If they can't on a continual basis, you will struggle with discipline in your sport. Your team will have more penalties and commit more unforced errors than the team who has the discipline to go on the whistle.

KIWI KAIZEN – 1% BETTER EACH DAY IN EVERYTHING

'Success leaves clues' and historically, the most successful professional team of any sport in the world is New Zealand's All Blacks rugby squad. They have a 77% winning record since 1903 in test match rugby play and are the only international club with a winning record against every opponent. Since the introduction of the World Rugby Rankings in 2003, the All Blacks have held the number one ranking longer than all other teams combined. What makes this success even more astounding is New Zealand is a nation of only four million people and they are playing a global schedule.

"Human beings are motivated by purpose, autonomy and a drive towards mastery. Accomplished leaders create an environment in which their people can develop their skills, their knowledge and their character. This leads to a learning environment and a culture of curiosity, innovation and continuous improvement. By finding the 100 things that can be done just 1 per cent better, leaders create incremental and cumulative advantage, and organizations see an upswing in performance and results. In creating a coherent learning environment, it pays to both eliminate unhelpful elements—clearing out the furniture—and to introduce insightful and inspiring influences." James Kerr, author of Legacy.

Kerr does an outstanding job of chronicling the All Blacks culture in his best-selling book. Key components of the All Blacks everything matters culture are:

1. **Champions do extra.** They find incremental ways to do more – in the weight room, on the field, or for the team. Exactly the point of this entire chapter, the All Blacks culture focuses on continual growth in every aspect of training. One great example is they all set their watches fast so they will always be early to

meetings. Their standard is 'do more than is expected' on everything.

2. **Leave the jersey better than you found it.** The All Blacks honor their past and realize the responsibility they have to continue to improve the history of the team. It gives them a higher purpose.

3. **Sweep the Shed.** This is one of the first stories I told the team after taking over at NF. Our locker room being clean on a daily basis was a continual struggle for Coach Bachtel and I so I wanted to let them know some of the most famous athletes in the world are not too good to pick up after themselves. The All Blacks have a 'no one should have to take care of us' mentality and the captains actually CLEAN THE LOCKER ROOM after everyone leaves post game. This would be like LeBron or Aaron Rogers waiting for all the reporters to clear out so they could grab a broom and tidy up so the janitors didn't have to do it.

4. **Better people make better All Blacks.** The local Maori custom of 'whanau' means extended family. The All Black standard does not tolerate those who do not follow this mantra. It does not matter how much potential a player has if he is not a team player he is not welcome. Each year some of the most talented young rugby players in New Zealand are not selected to join the team because management is not sold on their character.

Most of us have a professional or college team we are passionate about. How great would be if you knew your team had a culture similar to the All Blacks. Every year I love watching the NFL or NBA draft and every year I am amazed how little talk there is about the character

Culture Defeats Strategy 2 - Goonville, Texas Pop. 11

of the players. Everything measureable is analyzed and over-analyzed; height, weight, vertical jump, speed and quickness. Without fail, certain players' draft stock will rise after the season when they work out for teams' scouts and coaches because they tested better than expected.

I always wonder how much the intangibles factor into a teams' decision to take one player over another? When my team drafts a former team captain I am fired up. Captains are those you can count on, they are all in on the culture of their team. They can't live without the game. Count me in on those guys. The All Blacks feel the same way.

> *"It has been said that something as small as the flutter of a butterfly's wing can ultimately cause a typhoon halfway around the world."*
>
> **Chaos Theory**

THE BUTTERFLY EFFECT

Eric Luster, assistant head coach at NF, and I were talking about 'everything matters discipline' and how more experienced coaches are more likely to believe in it and understand it. "Most coaches make the mistake of being worried about immediate gratification. I was guilty of this as a young coach. Our staff was trying to win now and I was afraid if we didn't have this one player we wouldn't be successful for that week. It was a mistake to think this way. When you allow anyone to slide just a little on any of your core values the impact is not just on that week or that player. There is a ripple effect and it hurts your long-term success."

@CoachJacksonTPW   #culturematters

Culture Defeats Strategy 2 - Goonville, Texas Pop. 11

The lasting ripple Coach Luster mentioned in the quote above is brilliantly described by the theory of 'The Butterfly Effect.'

11/22/63 is one of Stephen King's most fascinating stories. It centers around a young man named Jake who discovers a portal in a pantry that leads back to 1958. Eventually, after a few visits to the portal, Jake decides he can alter history by preventing the assassination of President John F. Kennedy in 1963. He believes that if JFK is not killed it will greatly benefit the United States and all of humanity. In the portal and back in the past, Jake stalks Lee Harvey Oswald and manages to prevent him from shooting Kennedy.

> LEADERS ARE EXPOSED WHEN THEY HAVE TO GO THROUGH 'THE FIRE'. IF YOU BEND AND COMPROMISE WHEN THE CRISIS HITS DO NOT EXPECT YOUR TEAM TO BELIEVE YOU THE NEXT TIME YOU SAY 'THIS IS WHAT WE

Unfortunately, when he returns to the present instead of finding a world improved, Jake realizes the opposite has happened. His old home has been destroyed, earthquakes are much more common, and worst of all, nuclear war has destroyed much of the world. Distraught and saddened that his work in the past has done so much harm, he returns to 1958 to reset history.

The Urban Dictionary defines the butterfly effect as the scientific theory that a single occurrence, no matter how small, can change the course of the universe forever.

@CoachJacksonTPW #culturematters

Culture Defeats Strategy 2 - Goonville, Texas Pop. 11

1. A man travelled back in time to prehistoric ages and stepped on a butterfly, and the universe was entirely different when he got back.

2. The flap of a butterfly's wings changed the air around it so much that a tornado broke out two continents away.

The term 'butterfly effect' was coined in 1972 by Edward Lorenz who theorized a tornado (its exact time of formation and path taken) being influenced by minor variances in the atmosphere that could have been caused by the flapping of a butterfly's wings weeks ago and several thousand miles away.

> *"You could not remove a single grain of sand from its place without thereby...changing something throughout all parts of the immeasurable whole."*
>
> **Fichte, The Vocation of Man (1800)**

What does the butterfly effect have to do with changing a culture? Everything! Making sure your team is doing the little things every day is not a good thing, but mandatory. The color of the carpet is minutia that can bog down and even splinter organizations, but the daily fist-fight to make sure your athletes are finishing through the line is one of the things many coaches must deal with. Finishing a drill is the flap of the butterfly's wings that lead to the fumble or penalty we all know is the difference in a win or a loss.

@CoachJacksonTPW   #culturematters

LONG TERM COMPOUND INTEREST

Question: would you rather be given $5,000,000 or a single penny that doubled every day for a month? On first thought we would all probably say the $5 million but like all things we must factor in the long-term effects when we make any important decision.

I am not known for patience. Before I learned the impact of the benefit of compound interest I would have said quickly, 'give me the $5 million and let me go on my way'. It would have been a mistake because I wouldn't be allowing the money to grow with the power of compound interest.

Here is the staggering power of daily compound interest for a month;

Day 1: $.01
Day 2: $.02
Day 3: $.04
Day 4: $.08
Day 5: $.16
Day 6: $.32
Day 7: $.64
Day 8: $1.28
Day 9: $2.56
Day 10: $5.12
Day 11: $10.24
Day 12: $20.48
Day 13: $40.96
Day 14: $81.92
Day 15: $163.84
Day 16: $327.68
Day 17: $655.36
Day 18: $1,310.72

Day 19: $2,621.44
Day 20: $5,242.88
Day 21: $10,485.76
Day 22: $20,971.52
Day 23: $41,943.04
Day 24: $83,886.08
Day 25: $167,772.16
Day 26: $335,544.32
Day 27: $671,088.64
Day 28: $1,342,177.28
Day 29: $2,684,354.56
Day 30: $5,368,709.12

And...if we want to use a month with 31 days (who wouldn't), your doubled penny will become an astounding *$10,737,418.20!*

When you're taking over a program, take into account the benefit of laying the foundation of daily discipline. It will work just like compound interest if it's done DAILY. A leader can't pick and choose the issues to address and can't be in a certain mood to tackle the toughest problems because we aren't all in the right mood every day. Without consistency from the leader, an everything matters culture will not take hold.

HOMECOMING AT POTEET

Each team is going to face multiple crisis each season. Some will be unavoidable (injuries) and some will be self-inflicted (discipline issues). We faced a crisis at a critical part of our season and a decision had to be made.

Culture Defeats Strategy 2 - Goonville, Texas Pop. 11

I had to decide if I was going to stick a penny in the fuse box or stand firm and allow the compound interest to grow. The incident we dealt with happened to us before we played at Mesquite Poteet. Not only was it the first time for me to coach against a team I have very fond memories of leading for three years, but the game was also their homecoming. The crowd was large and it was an important district contest for both sides. We were 4-1 overall coming in, 1-1 in district play. We had just lost at Highland Park, where it was close in the fourth quarter the week before. We desperately needed a win to get back the momentum and juice we created by starting the season 4-0.

During our week of practice one of our offensive starters broke a school and team rule that went against our standard and core values. I had a decision to make — suspend him or punish him in the pit of misery for a few days and let him play? It wasn't a hard call for me. I've been down this road before and knew if I was going to stand up and say to our team, 'this is how we do things and we aren't changing our standard for you,' then I'd better back it up, or lose a lot of credibility. If I had let him play and not sat him down for the game, the rest of the season, and even the next few years at NF to some extent would have caused players to think 'he may not hold me accountable if I am one of our best players.'

Culture Defeats Strategy 2 - Goonville, Texas Pop. 11

Everything matters, but especially the word of the leader. Have standards and values, emphasize them every day and stick to your guns when the crisis occurs (and it always does). To make matters worse, one of our best offensive linemen, John Taylor, was injured the day before the game so we had to shuffle the big boys for the first time on very short notice. We played well at Poteet and beat them 40-28. Our defense played its best game of the year and made big stops when they had to. One of our offensive starters, tight end Barclay Ford, began going 'both ways' and playing defensive end this game. He had a key interception of a screen pass. Calvin Ribera (pictured) rushed for 246 yards and two touchdowns to carry our offense and eat up the clock in the fourth quarter. It was the first victory ever for NF vs. the Pirates. It was so satisfying for me because I know what a great program head coach Kody Groves runs and more importantly, it put us 2-1 in district play and back in the driver's seat to make the playoffs in a very tough league.

When you're going through a crisis, you must stand your ground if the issue is going to compromise the culture you are trying so hard to create. The spring before (Chapter 1) was a massive daily struggle and although we weren't dealing with issues nearly as often, we still had some bad habits and couldn't look the other way. The ultimate test of the leader's fortitude is playing time vs. a district opponent. Although it's easy to tell this story now, the week of game was not nearly as comfortable. I desperately wanted to win but not enough to sacrifice my character and message to the vast majority who had gotten in our wheelbarrow.

The most satisfying part of the story is the suspended player had a great week of practice in every way. His

@CoachJacksonTPW #culturematters

Culture Defeats Strategy 2 - Goonville, Texas Pop. 11

attitude, effort, and 'coachability' were the best since we arrived at North. When I suspend a player, they're still required to dress for the game. At times, they can bring an attitude that can be less than team-oriented but he was one of our greatest encouragers on the sideline the entire time. He didn't pout and feel sorry for himself but helped us win with his juice and team-first demeanor. It was also the last issue we had with this young man. He went on a great run and was a beast for us from the last three weeks of the regular season and our three playoff games. The last six weeks were so impressive he was offered a football scholarship and signed in February. The lesson of holding him accountable not only helped us enforce our culture, but was a teachable moment for him and will greatly enhance his chance of succeeding in the 'dog eat dog' world of college football.

> *"Practice the philosophy of continual improvement. Get a little bit better every single day."*
>
> Brian Tracy

When a rocket ship takes off it requires 75% of its energy to get it off the ground and into orbit. Once the vessel is cruising in the earth's atmosphere it still requires energy but getting it outside the earth's gravitational pull is the most stressful on the engines. When you're taking over a program, don't compromise the 'now' for the long-term. When you do this, you're not only enabling your people – which will hurt them in the future – but you'll keep your team from winning the close games most of the time. Your team will not have the discipline and attention to detail needed to outplay an opponent without an 'everything matters' foundation.

@CoachJacksonTPW   #culturematters

CHAPTER 2 REVIEW
'EVERYTHING MATTERS'

- [ ] The little things matter because EVERYTHING MATTERS.

- [ ] 100% is much easier than 99%. Pennies in the fuse box will get you beat.

- [ ] To have 'bright lines' of accountability you must have systems in place.

- [ ] 'Count On Me' priorities give your players or anyone in an organization what is an excused or unexcused absence.

- [ ] The All Blacks are a great example of an 'everything matters' culture.

- [ ] Stand your ground when there is (and there inevitably will be) a challenge to your culture. Just like raising your own children, stay consistent.

CHAPTER 3
LESSON #2 - THE DAILY FIST-FIGHT

> *"Coach, you're telling me you meet with your team every day for 15 minutes or more and don't ever talk about football?"*
>
> **Craig Bennet**
> **Head Football Coach**
> **Camden H.S. Georgia**

Six recruits of the elite spy group called the Kingsman are free falling rapidly after jumping from a plane when their instructor, Merlin, tells them one of the six jumpers does not have a working parachute. They must work together and figure out a way to get all six down safely. They've all jumped several times in training so for most there is no immediate panic as they decide to join hands and team up to figure out their next move. The stress builds quickly ask *they're falling at a rate of 120 mph.*

Within a few seconds one of the jumpers can't stand it any longer and pulls his cord to see if he is the one in danger. He is thrust hundreds of feet in the air as his chute opens. The others close in and all grab hands. They're working as a team, it seems

Culture Defeats Strategy 2 - Goonville, Texas Pop. 11

and are finding a way to stay together. 'Beep!' - a low altitude sensor goes off in each of their headsets and quickly another recruit bails by pulling his cord. Now there are four and they are falling fast. The tension builds as the music gets louder. The cameras show the immense stress on each of their faces. Another recruit says 'uncle' and pulls his cord.

They're down to three and only two have working parachutes. In their helmets, the warning buzzer has sounded, reminding them of the impending danger. One of the top candidates, Charlie, pulls his handle to see if he's the one. He's also shot up in the air when his parachute opens.

The two main heroines - Roxy and Eggsy - are left and have but a few precious seconds to figure it out or one of them is going to splatter all over the English countryside.

*Eggsy yells to Roxy, "no matter what happens now, I've got you," as he grabs her tight and makes sure they will not let go of each other. The music gets more intense the closer they get to hitting the groun*d. *Merlin is so nervous he knocks his coffee cup off his desk, breaking it. The radar is showing 500 feet - 400 feet - 300 feet when Roxy goes first and pulls the handle of her parachute ... it opens! Eggsy hangs on for all he's worth. He manages to barely keep his grip as the they tumble to the ground! The*

@CoachJacksonTPW   #culturematters

suspenseful scene with the music and drama ends as they lay next to each other grasping for breath.

Coach PJ Fleck used this video clip when he presented to the coaches of the Minnesota Football Coaches Association in April of 2018. I had the great fortune to be invited to participate as a speaker so I was in the audience taking it all in as Coach Fleck led us through how he structures his daily team meetings.

"We will always use short videos to hold their attention and help us make our point. Each day we're going to show them a movie clip, a highlight of a sporting event or a current event from the news to help drive our message home," said Coach Fleck.

I have always been proud of the job coaches in our programs have done of meeting with our teams on a daily basis. The first time I got very intentional about it was in 2010 at Mesquite Poteet. We were on 90-minute block class periods and the rule in Texas is you can only use 60-minutes to work out each day no matter what bell schedule your school is using. Schools on block schedule have 30 'extra' minutes each day that needs to be some type of study hall or even better, leadership development.

We purchased the Growing Leaders' Habitudes program to give us a curriculum to follow. Habitudes does an amazing job of teaching life lessons through visual stories. I'm a firm believer it was one of the ingredients in the recipe that helped us take a 1-19 program to 12-3 the first year. It, of course, was only a portion of it but there's no doubt in my mind getting together as a team helped us bond and gave me and our coaches a platform to talk to them about things other than football.

Over the years, I've gotten better as a presenter and teacher in our leadership development time, but Coach Fleck's demonstration of implementing movie clips was a game-changer for me. In the original Culture Defeats Strategy, I mention Pete Carroll's philosophy of 'fascinating' his Seahawks daily. The parachute clip from the movie Kingsman grabbed me and still does even after I've used it and watched the drama several times myself while teaching seminars.

In this chapter, we will discuss the structure of and key ways to have elite position meetings and team meetings. I will attempt to sell you on the absolute necessity for you to get in the 'daily fist-fight' required to build a solid foundation for *your championship culture*.

THE MOST COMMON MISTAKE

Recently, I've begun to do a few one-day seminars to help coaches build their own championship culture called The Culture Factory. It has been a blessing to travel and meet outstanding

> IF YOU WILL COMMIT TO DAILY LEADERSHIP TIME YOUR PROGRAM WILL BE IN THE TOP 1% NATIONALLY IN CREATING A CULTURE.

coaches with growth mindsets who are looking to get the edge. It's also a huge honor to be trusted to meet with their staffs and have coaches spend precious resources to take care of my flight, hotel, and stipend.

Culture Defeats Strategy 2 - Goonville, Texas Pop. 11

Some of the most respected coaches who know a lot more football than I ever will have been in the audience. Here is the biggest take-home for me after several 'Factory' events: most programs have some form of core values but aren't stressing or emphasizing them on a regular basis ... or at all. Getting people from different walks of life, socio-economic backgrounds, different skill levels and different goals to think, speak, and act the same is a tough task and can only happen if it's done daily. Just like bathing every day is much more effective than once a week. I wash daily and it works pretty well. Our daily system of culture works pretty well also.

Another key to the daily fist fight is we must prepare a lesson just like in a typical classroom because we are trying to achieve the same goal of a classroom teacher. We call our time with them our 'Leadership Academy.' It's a classroom for all things Goonville culture. We are teaching our program's values and standards so we cannot just go in and 'wing it.' Standing and delivering a speech isn't going to be any more effective than it would be for Josh McCown, one of our receiver coaches who is also a high school math teacher. Like most teachers, Coach McCown works hard each night getting ready to teach his students. He's on a mission to 'get this concept taught' so he can build on it and next week 'get that concept taught.' It doesn't happen by accident. His students take a state assessment exam in early May and he knows has to attack each day in September, October, etc. for his students' scores to be high. It's the same with an intentional culture for any program. I spend quite a bit of time on each lesson but give our coaches an advance schedule for our weekly topics. Before the season, each coach has chosen his topic so

@CoachJacksonTPW #culturematters

there is no reason me and our staff can't take our time and make each day a fascinatingly *effective lesson.*

HOW WE LEARN

We create the classroom environment each day where we are 100% teaching things other than football. Since we are teaching we need to understand how humans learn. I haven't been in an academic classroom since 2008 when I taught U.S. Government at Lone Oak High School in Lone Oak, Texas. I began my career in 1990 and I 'stood and delivered' to students for several years. I took my job as a teacher seriously and never 'mailed it in.' My students *learned the material but I wish I had been using the system we use now for our team meetings.*

Academic classroom strategies were starting to shift to more of a student-centered learning style a*bout the time I was leaving the classroom and being allowed to focus on my athletic director and head football coaching duties full time. Lecture style teaching was being phased out. The norm of presenting, then assign homework, then check for understanding, was fading away.*

In the spring of *1995 I was interviewing for an assistant coaching position at Atlanta High School* in Atlanta, Texas. *The head coach and I were talking when an assistant coach entered and said, "coach, can I have the topic to discuss with the team for today?" The head coach grabbed* a small *daily flip calendar with a leadership quote or thought on it and handed it to the assistant. I was very impressed that they spoke to their team each day about a topic of personal growth and character. It was the first time I'd ever witnessed a program having a system and* using precious minutes of offseason *to do this. They were ahead of their time and sadly this strategy would still be better than most programs are doing now.*

This method of character development will help you give your group a few minutes of non-sports leadership training. It's certainly better than not doing any leadership activity with your team *but you get what you invest so the return will also be minimal.*

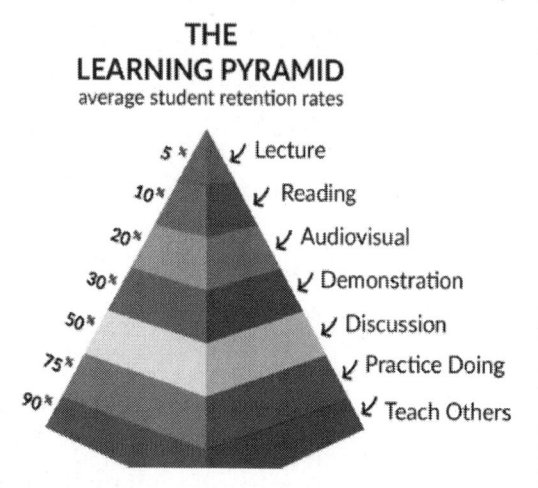

THE LEARNING PYRAMID
average student retention rates

- 5% Lecture
- 10% Reading
- 20% Audiovisual
- 30% Demonstration
- 50% Discussion
- 75% Practice Doing
- 90% Teach Others

At North Forney, we're going to take it to a level not matched by many. It's a systematic daily approach anyone can do if they are willing to spend the time beforehand and willing to get home a few minutes later each evening because practice started 10-15 minutes past the time it used to begin.

BE A DIRECT TEACHER AND NOT A PRESENTER

YouTube is arguably the greatest teaching tool ever invented. Millions of videos are uploaded each day covering every subject known the man. A few years ago, I ran across a video of Urban Meyer addressing the 2012 Ohio High School Football Coaches Association. Coach Meyer's presentation is 60 minutes of gold as he describes how they teach the Buckeye players in position meetings. Every couple of years I ask our coaches to watch the video and we discuss it in our July preparation meetings.

> "Each Thanksgiving my sister, who is a provost at the University of Cincinnati, and I get in an argument about whether she's a teacher or a presenter. I say she's a presenter. She gives the information to each class and if they get it, they pass. If they don't, they fail. At Ohio State, our coaches will be direct teachers, they will not just give information but thoroughly and actively check for understanding in their unit meetings. It's not what our coaches know, but what our players know."
> (quote from the 2012 presentation to Ohio H.S. football coaches)
>
> **Urban Meyer**
> **Former NCAA Head Football Coach**

There are so many 'take-homes' from Coach Meyer's presentation but the quote above is #1 for me. He's calling all of us out who have sat on our butts with our position groups or our teams and just ran the clicker back and forth. I used to do it and it happens every day across the world. Stop - rewind - correct - play - make a point about a technique - stop - rewind - correct ... you get the idea.

A great classroom teacher doesn't sit at their desk, or stand at a podium, give their students the information and 'hope for the best.' They're actively moving around and engaging everyone in the room. They're using 'call backs' (we will discuss later), video clips and everything they can from the learning pyramid. They're teaching because they have a heart for it and in most places, are held accountable if their students learn the information.

THE ELITE LEARNING ENVIRONMENT

Does it matter when or where you have your leadership time? Of course, it does - Everything matters! We have a large area we carved out of our weight room (we actually call our weight room the 'Collision Enhancement Center') to meet with our guys each day. They sit in rows of 'battalions'. We have them sit with their legs crossed in front and eyes forward.

"We used to put 60 athletes in a classroom with guys just hanging all over themselves but it wasn't a great environment. It was too casual," Dane Oliver, head football coach at Missoula Sentinel High School told me once. I totally agree with him. We should think military or Division 1 college program and ask ourselves how close we can get to how they meet and teach. The facilities at NF are terrific and I'm grateful. We have an indoor facility most coaches would kill to have but, like 99% of the high schools in America, we don't have a formal meeting space for 125 athletes.

We don't focus on what we don't have. We focus on getting it done and we do this on a rubber floor space with a white board and TV overhead. Our guys are locked in, they participate because we're intentional about it and demand that they do just like any classroom teacher would require.

I asked for some feedback for this chapter from the few coaches who were with us during my first spring at NF. I asked them what they remembered of our leadership lessons the first spring. "They were excited to hear who you were going to talk about that day," said assistant coach Brayden MaQuar. "They had never been exposed to the format of a pre-practice meeting before. None of them had heard of Jocko, the All Blacks, or David Goggins. It was powerful teaching for them."

It took a while to get them in my normal routine of how we would meet each day. I'll never forget after about a week and they started feeling a little comfortable someone would literally break wind while I was teaching a lesson. The first time I ignored it thinking it surely was an accident. There were a few giggles but it didn't derail the lesson. A few days later it happened again. With almost 100 bodies sitting close to each other it was impossible for me to know who thought this was a good idea. In Chapter 1, I mentioned during my first meeting in the auditorium with the principal, athletic director and assistant superintendent present, I had to ask them twice not to talk while I was talking. The program was going nowhere until we could all sit down and act like a team. So, what did I do the second time I was interrupted by what was now definitely on-purpose rudeness? I did what I always do and what you must always do - I addressed it.

Culture Defeats Strategy 2 - Goonville, Texas Pop. 11

This wasn't a 'it's not your fault moment.' This was a culture of disrespect that had to be dealt with. "Who in here can't sit for 20 minutes without interrupting me by breaking wind and trying to get attention? If we need to instill more discipline before we can meet or if we need to remove one of you from the program so we can talk to the team we will. I am fine with either but we are going to stand in front of you each day and talk about what the North Forney Falcon football program is going to be about without interruptions. This is not optional and is not a request. If you have a medical condition where you can't control yourself for an extended period of time let me know, otherwise the next time will be bad for the team." We didn't have another issue.

The take-home I hope you get from this story is you can make this happen if you are committed. Your team will eventually love this system but it'll be new to them, so you will have to have clear expectations and be willing to hold them accountable.

KEEP THEM ON EDGE

I attended a teacher in-service over 20-years ago and learned the correct way to pose a question to a class. This may seem like overkill to some but it's a big deal to use the proper technique when calling on a group for an answer. Some instructors will do it this way, "Bob, what is the square root of 150?" This isn't how to do it. What's wrong with this technique? As soon as the word 'Bob' comes out of your mouth everyone else in the room will; 1. relieved they don't have to answer it, and 2. May start thinking about something they are going to do after school. The way to keep them on edge is to ask it this way, "What is the square root of 150? ... pause a few seconds so everyone is computing it in their head and then call on someone ... "Bob?"

When you're in an athletic setting it works the same way. Ask the group, "what is our go-to inbounds play vs. man defense under our basket?" Pause for a moment and ask for an answer from a specific player.

Another way to keep them on their toes is to ask questions frequently and ones that require concise, one- or two-word answers. An elite teacher or coach (they are both the same) will constantly keep the group engaged by firing off questions to everyone in the group regardless of their playing time.

When I was in Minnesota for the MFCA clinic, we were invited to attend position meetings and watch a spring practice. As always, I went to the offensive line meeting. **Coach Brian Callahan** was masterful at creating a supreme learning environment. He kept every player engaged. He stood up the entire time and asked at least three questions for every play they watched from the film. The questions were rapid-fire and involved everyone in the room. Before the ball is snapped the film is paused, "The play is 32 zone. What call are we making when the backer walks up in 'A' gap? George?" "Alpha," George responded quickly. Coach Callahan now pushes play for about a second and then pauses it as it is just developing. "Is this a good call versus 'A' gap blitz ... Casey?" "Yes sir, if we stay on our tracks," he answers. "What step should we take on the play side ... Brandon?" "Full bucket, but I have to get my second step to his crotch to have any power," says Brandon. You might be thinking, 'does it take too long to go through film this way?' It's quick, but more importantly it's awesome. I would give up being a little slower with this system than doing it the way most do where the coach is sitting on this butt and the players are working hard to stay awake because he's just talking through each play.

Another great technique Coach Callahan used was including every single player in the room. Don't get me wrong, coaches must know if the first-teamers are ready to go, but the future starters and injured players will 'die on the vine' if they are ignored day after day. Be intentional about engaging everyone in your position meetings.

> *"When do you know your team is ready? When they not only know what they are doing but why they're doing it."*
>
> **Bill Parcells**

I'm all in on the quote above describing when you know your team is ready to go. How do you find out if they know what to do and why they're doing it? Stand them up and put them on the whiteboard. Have them draw what their assignment is and the players next to them, if they can.

The push-up game - Coach Bret Brown of the Philadelphia 76ers calls on a player and gets him on the board to diagram a play. For example, "Steve, draw up our first inbounds play when we're under our own basket?" Steve is allowed one 'life-line' to help him but if they fail to draw up the correct play, both are doing a few push-ups. The best part of the game to keep everyone engaged is if they do nail it and get it right, then the coaches must do the push-ups.

Not only is this 'on-edge' teaching but 'on-edge' learning. When I read the article about Coach Brown's push-up game the actual player who drew up the play was lottery pick Ben Simmons. He's one of their best players, but was injured at the time and would not be healthy for a few more weeks. This is a terrific example of keeping everyone on edge and involved with the team, players and coaches.

"JUICE OR NO JUICE?"

Callbacks are essential to keeping your team engaged. At times during your meeting, ask them a familiar question that they can all shout out easily but also helps drive home one of your core values. Some we use are:

"Tough or soft?" **"TOUGH!"**
"Elite or average?" **"ELITE!"**
"Family or selfish?" **"FAMILY!"**
"Juice or no juice?" **"JUICE!"**

I had to put a picture of callbacks in my presentations to remind me to do this early on but I have continued to use the graphics for the visual reinforcement as well.

> *"If you don't feel it you won't remember it."*
> Bob Dickman

FACTS TELL - STORIES SELL

Our brains are hardwired to remember stories. The human mind is a story-processor, not a logic or information-processor. When we hear a tale that involves someone or someplace we can relate to, large areas of our brain are activated and firing.

Jesus taught in parables to make his message resonate with his audiences. A parable is described as an earthly story with a heavenly meaning. Using parables allowed Jesus to present clear stories from everyday events that the crowd could understand because the stories created imagery in their brains.

The parable of the Good Samaritan - Luke 10:29-37

[29] so he asked Jesus, "And who is my neighbor?"

[30] In reply Jesus said: "A man was going down from Jerusalem to Jericho, when he was attacked by robbers. They stripped him of his clothes, beat him and went away, leaving him half dead. [31] A priest happened to be going down the same road, and when he saw the man, he passed by on the other side. [32] So too, a Levite, when he came to the place and saw him, passed by on the other side. [33] But a **Samaritan**, as he

Culture Defeats Strategy 2 - Goonville, Texas Pop. 11

traveled, came where the man was; and when he saw him, he took pity on him. [34] He went to him and bandaged his wounds, pouring on oil and wine. Then he put the man on his own donkey, brought him to an inn and took care of him. [35] The next day he took out two denarii and gave them to the innkeeper. 'Look after him,' he said, 'and when

I return, I will reimburse you for any extra expense you may have.'

[36] "Which of these three do you think was a neighbor to the man who fell into the hands of robbers?"

[37] The expert in the law replied, **"The one who had mercy on him."**

Jesus told him, **"Go and do likewise."**

This is Jesus' version of using media through a story for his audience. It's very similar to you and I using a movie clip to help our team greater understand our point. His teachings were totally unconventional for the time and although many were listening because of initial excitement, they might reject the word as unintelligible if he were to speak to them as an academic. It would be like Albert Einstein explaining the theory of relativity to me in a lecture situation, but if he were to use a movie clip from 'Back to the Future' and compare it with the flux capacitor, I'd have a chance to grasp the basics.

> **"The power of story is atomic. It's the one thing that can hold our attention for hours."**
> **Bob Dickman**

The Four Components of a Story

Dave Lieber, columnist for the *Fort Worth Star-Telegram*, gave an excellent presentation for a TEDx talk titled, 'The Power of Storytelling to Change the World.' Lieber begins the talk by telling his struggle of a Jewish man moving from New York and his tough transition to conservative Texas.

He does a great job pulling his audience into his world. Lieber uses some humor to tell why he moved to Fort Worth, and his struggle to get his readers to connect with a new outsider. "My columns were not very popular early and I wasn't sure a Jew from New York was going to make it in Texas."
He then goes into how he met a local woman, how they fell in love and his decision to go against advice from his editor and propose to her in one of his columns.

Now, his readers believe this New Yorker is a normal person like them and his column began to gain a lot of traction. His personal life and professional life turned 180 degrees and 24 years later, all is still great for him.

From the beginning, Lieber had my attention. I was empathic to his story of being an outsider and was rooting for him to 'get his girl.' It was a great Ted talk because it had the four components of all stories, which was the actual reason he was speaking.

Lieber's 4 Components of all Stories:
1. Introduce the main character or protagonist.
2. The protagonist has a crisis.
3. The protagonist overcomes the crisis and succeeds.

Culture Defeats Strategy 2 - Goonville, Texas Pop. 11

4. Storyteller ties up the loose ends with closure. The French word for this is the 'denouement.'

When your team is on a losing streak or faces a serious crisis, remind them your season is a story. All the epic stories have the dip down. It will take some protagonists (captains) to get the team to stay the course, get the line of the story to shoot back up and tie up all the loose ends. The famous 'process' we talk about in our program is the daily crisis - or Sisyphus' pushing the rock (the downward line). If we take care of attacking the dip down, our success and denouement will take care of itself.

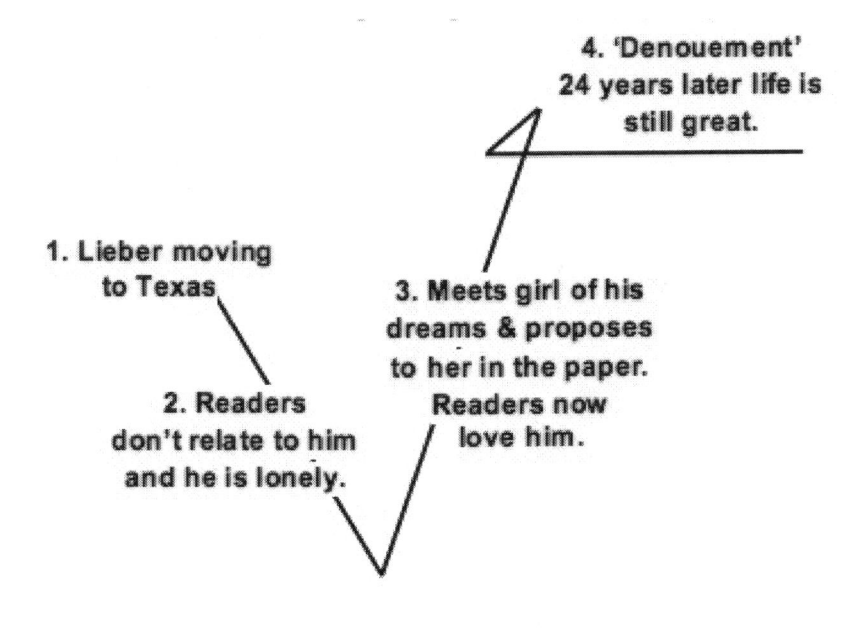

4. 'Denouement'
24 years later life is still great.

1. Lieber moving to Texas

3. Meets girl of his dreams & proposes to her in the paper. Readers now love him.

2. Readers don't relate to him and he is lonely.

@CoachJacksonTPW   #culturematters

USE MEDIA TO FASCINATE THEM AND MAKE THE POINT

In addition to hearing Coach Fleck present to all the coaches at the Minnesota Football Coaches Association, I was able to sit in on a University of Minnesota football team meeting the next morning. I took notes on everything and when arriving back to Texas made a few tweaks to our daily 'fist-fight.' Coach Fleck's key point in his presentation to the coaches on Friday was the power of media – especially video clips from movies – when speaking to your team. I will forever be grateful for being allowed to see it first-hand the next morning. It was an event more than a meeting.

As I entered the team room, the Bruno Mars song, '24 Karat Magic' was playing loud. It was looped to play continuously until Coach Fleck entered the room. The music was an intentional tactic to infuse some 'juice' to his guys early on a Saturday morning. *Side note- when he did come in, the players yelled and gave him a standing ovation. I was told it happens every day. It was powerful and I knew I was in for something special over the next 30 minutes.

Several areas of the Gophers' core values were addressed that morning, but the two where he used video clips still stand out to me.

1. Discipline – "Men, we will be tough, edgy but will always have discipline," Coach Fleck said to them. He then discussed LeBron James, who he considers having an edge but always in command of his emotions. "I'm sure all of you know what legendary MMA fighter Connor McGregor decided to do this week

Culture Defeats Strategy 2 - Goonville, Texas Pop. 11

in New York." As he is saying this a video begins to play of McGregor going onto to a bus and trying to fight a fellow MMA athlete. When he can't get this done he eventually finds a hand-truck or two-wheeler and throws it through one of the bus windows. He was basically out of control and quickly arrested. "We are going to be LeBron James, in control. Teams that have guys like Connor McGregor we will beat because they can't control themselves when the game is on the line."

2. Result and Response - "How many in here know who Sergio Garcia is?" Surprising to me only six or so raised their hands. "He's one of the best golfers in the world", Coach Fleck told them. "Last year he won arguably the most prestigious tournament of the year when he won the Masters." A picture of him holding up the trophy and wearing the green jacket is on the screen. "The Masters is being played again this week and Sergio was defending his title but didn't make the cut."

A video of him begins to play. It's Sergio during his infamous '13' shot hole just the day before. "Men, one of the greatest golfers in the world, a man who is the reigning champ, is having one of the worst holes in the history of professional golf. I want you to watch the crowd. Look at everyone begin to laugh as he hits ball after ball in the water. Even little kids are laughing at a Top 10 golfer in the world."

@CoachJacksonTPW #culturematters

Culture Defeats Strategy 2 - Goonville, Texas Pop. 11

"I want us to focus on his response. He doesn't have a temper-tantrum. He doesn't throw his club or curse at his caddy. Garcia keeps his cool and finishes the hole with outstanding body language. Coach Fleck now posts a picture of all of Garcia's shots are on the screen giving us all, especially the 95% who don't play golf, a terrific visual of how many times he actually hit the ball in the water.

"Does anyone happen to know what he does the next hole? He birdied it. Think about much mental toughness this required. He just had the worst hole of his career and is not going to make the cut and defend his title. People who couldn't play within 50 shots of him were laughing at him. He not only kept his composure on that hole but more impressively regrouped and had an elite response. Most professional golfers wouldn't have the toughness to do this. The very next hole he played his best hole of the day."

Every coach in the world has had the issue of players getting down when adversity strikes. In the original Culture Defeats Strategy, I wrote that a great definition of mental toughness is how quickly one can 'shake it off' or 'snap and clear' and play the next play. If Coach Fleck had talked about Sergio's disaster on hole 15 and then the masterful 16th hole the day before without video, it would not have had near the impact.

@CoachJacksonTPW #culturematters

Culture Defeats Strategy 2 - Goonville, Texas Pop. 11

This picture I snapped on a flight coming back from Edmonton, Canada. Here are two kids sitting across from each other who are not traveling together, and not quite old enough to speak conversationally with each other. The boy might be four years old and I am guessing the girl is a few months younger, probably closer to three.

I wasn't paying attention to them until I noticed him taking her picture and then editing it by adding flowers in her hair (his mom helped him get to the correct screen) and a dog nose to her face. They never said one word to each other but their attention stayed on the same thing (the phone) for around five minutes. You can see from the look on his face he is totally engaged. He is in his element! If you want to fascinate and reach your players you must use some technology!

TRANSFER PASSION

The last aspect that must take place to really reach your players or students is they must feel your passion. You can do everything mentioned in this chapter, have a supreme learning environment, use great stories, find video and movie clips that are spot on but it will not be true teaching unless you are 'bringing it' with some juice from the heart.

Culture Defeats Strategy 2 - Goonville, Texas Pop. 11

Recently I finished a workout at the end of the day at Orange Theory Fitness (a great system to get a total workout and have someone lead you through it). As I was walking through the lobby, there were several young men and women along with the owner, Brett. I could tell they weren't normal 'Team Orange' members, customers like me. He told me they were potential coaches about to audition to join one of his franchises.

It was not my place to say anything to the group so I didn't. But in my mind, I was thinking, "it's not about your knowledge of technique. A great coach finds a way to let others feel their passion for fitness. Transfer the love from your heart to our heart and everyone will want you to coach them."

That's what it's all about for anyone teaching anything. Students need to feel you love what you are teaching. Coach Fleck brought the juice in his presentation to coaches on Friday night and exactly the same amount of passion the next morning as he was leading his team.

At the MFCA clinic I have mentioned a couple of times earlier I sat very near some 'veteran high school coaches' from Minnesota at a social on the first night of the clinic immediately following Coach Fleck's presentation. I couldn't help but hear one of them refer to Coach Fleck as 'P.J. Flake.' I couldn't believe my ears. I had just sat in on 55 minutes of greatness and they were not speaking highly of him. I couldn't resist so I asked, "what is it about Coach Fleck you don't like?" One of the coaches responded, "it's not our style here in Minnesota. He seems like he is going to win by smoke and mirrors and football is a game of

Culture Defeats Strategy 2 - Goonville, Texas Pop. 11

blocking and tackling." I am typing this in December of 2019 and the UM football team has had magical season. They are 10-2 and will play in a relevant bowl game. I wonder what the 'old guys' in Minnesota think now?

I understand this is not for everybody. One of my favorite quotes is 'greatness is overrated'. It means it takes A LOT of work that most aren't willing to put in to be great. Most of you reading this won't do a daily team meeting and that's ok, but at least you know one of the reasons P.J. Fleck turns around programs and wins BIG.

LEADERSHIP ACADEMY IN GOONVILLE, TEXAS

Let's put a denouement on this chapter with an example of how we will take all this and teach our Falcon culture.

Each week we have a lesson topic that will be important to our motto for that quarter. In this example, I will use 'BE REMEMBERED.' We also use our core values for a week every year when we get back in January, but for the most part our message titles are more specific and we tie in our core values. Titles of lessons we did last year were: Body Language and Eye Contact, Kaizen, Identity, Elite, and Leaders Eat Last, to name a few.

The 'Academy' setting: Our goons arrive around 6:30 a.m. to a song playing in our hallway that reinforces the core value of the day. For example: Wednesday is blue collar tough so we have 'Tough Enough' by the Fabulous Thunderbirds looped continuously. They will hear it anytime they enter or exit the locker rooms from 6:30 to 9:30 a.m. when they are heading to 2nd period class. After they get dressed for workout they meet with their position or unit coach so he can check roll for attendance.

I blow the whistle at 6:50 and the coaches dismiss their groups to get their notebook, pen and align in the proper row. Any coach not presenting is in the back making sure everyone is paying attention and locked in. We are trying to achieve the ultimate learning environment as much as possible. We have a 60-inch television above a white board to show a power point presentation and movie clips.

THE LESSON - 'BE REMEMBERED'

The song 'Remember the Name' by Fort Minor is playing in our leadership area as they enter and meet with their coach. We're trying to use every part of the learning pyramid possible.

I begin with a 'callback'. It is Monday (Juice is our core value) so I ask, "Juice or No Juice?" "JUICE!," they respond with enthusiasm.

Culture Defeats Strategy 2 - Goonville, Texas Pop. 11

I begin my power point with a slide of a collage of players from college and professional football holding up a trophy. "Leave a legacy. What does this mean to you?" Someone raises their hand and after I call on him says, "What you accomplish when you are here."

> **KNOW YOUR AUDIENCE. IF YOUR TEAM DOES NOT LOOK FORWARD TO THE DAILY LEADERSHIP TIME, YOU MUST FIND WAYS TO MAKE IT HAPPEN**

Another says, "What people will say about you or your team one day."

"Yes, I agree," I say. "For me, my definition is how you and your team will be remembered after you are finished playing. Everyone wants to be a hero but not many are remembered for years after they play. We are going to talk this week about being remembered and what is required for that to happen." This is an easy lesson to go through here because I do believe every high school player wants to be a hero and be remembered.

Another callback. This one they haven't heard before but as you will see they are so easy it doesn't matter. "Remembered or forgotten?" "REMEMBERED!"

Now the really good stuff that captures them- a movie clip. This one from the movie 'Troy.' The protagonist in the story is Achilles. It's a perfect story to sell our 'Be Remembered' theme for the week. Achilles has a strange fate hanging over him. He has two choices: Choice #1 is to fight in the Trojan War and become a hero, but die young. Choice #2 is to stay out of the war and live a long life, but without glory. So, in our terms, he can be remembered forever and leave a

Culture Defeats Strategy 2 - Goonville, Texas Pop. 11

legacy or not work hard, not do what it takes and not embrace our core value of competition and be forgotten. Boom.

<u>20-second clip</u> - A boy is sent by the king to go find Achilles and bring him to fight Boagrius, a massive warrior (think Goliath) of an opposing tribe. As Achilles is mounting his horse the boy says, "I wouldn't want to fight a man that size." Achilles calmly and frankly replies, "That's why no one will remember your name" and then rides off.

This scene is perfect to reinforce our message of the week. As you will see, it is important to use short clips and discuss them. Do not take for granted they are understanding exactly why you are using it to teach. I will pause and ask questions if the clip is over 30 seconds.

<u>5-second clip</u> - Achilles is shown riding up to the battle scene. All of the Thessalonian troops are cheering him on. "He can be the hero," I tell them.

<u>5-second clip</u> - Boagrius is yelling and flexing his muscles to his fellow troops. I ask, "What does this represent when we are playing?" No one has a guess so I tell them, "This is like when we're playing a team that is making a lot of noise or even taunting us before the game."

<u>20-second clip</u> - Achilles is now ready and begins to run at Boagrius. I paused it to ask, "What is he doing right now that is much like how we play?" Again, not much of an answer which is fine because it is about me being able to make a point and sell our culture. "He is attacking. We do the same thing on defense

@CoachJacksonTPW 86 #culturematters

when we run to the ball. We attack relentlessly on offense with our tempo. Every time we attempt an onside kick we're attacking like Achilles. Boagrius is throwing spears at him but he doesn't care. He's attacking anyway."

I hit play again. Achilles finishes his attack by closing in on Boagrius, jumping in the air when he gets on him and stabbing him at the base of the neck. Boagrius stands still for a second and then falls forward, dead. Achilles' army goes crazy.

20-second clip - Achilles walks to the enemy side and yells to the group of soldiers, "Is there no one else? Is there no one else?" The enemy king asks him, "Who are you?" Achilles replies, "I am Achilles, son of the goddess Nereid Thetis." Now, comes the greatest denouement of all time as the king responds to him with, "I will remember the name." Boom! If you can't see the greatness of using these clips to teach your team how to be remembered then you may need to get out of coaching (just joking but not really).

After the clips, I close out the classroom portion of the lesson and we get in small groups, 'family groups,' as we call them. Each coach will have 10-12 in his family. They spread out in designated areas to discuss the lesson of the day. The coach who presented the main lesson (I do about 50% and the staff splits up the other 50%) has two or three questions to facilitate. His main goal is not to talk the entire time but to get his group talking. We spend 7-8 minutes in our small group time. Sometimes we actually do this in the middle of practice. We have it scripted as 'halftime.' It gives our guys a small break during practice and we definitely have their full attention.

Culture Defeats Strategy 2 – Goonville, Texas Pop. 11

<u>Family group discussion questions</u>:
1. We know Achilles killed Boagrius and it made him a hero to his people. What was the #1 tactic he used to defeat a man so much larger?

2. Have you ever been part of a team that was an underdog but was victorious? If so how did you win? Have you ever personally won although you were the underdog in a 1v1 individual competition?

3. How is this story something we can use this week when we think about our legacy?

Other ways to teach 'Be Remembered'

TUESDAY - 'Down the Stretch' – The movie Seabiscuit has lots of great teachable moments we can use to reinforce leaving a legacy and being remembered.

Show a clip of Seabiscuit's injury and all he had to overcome. Not only was he 'washed up,' but his jockey was injured and told he would never race again. Finish with his owner finally getting fellow horse War Admiral to race and Seabiscuit defeating the much bigger horse.

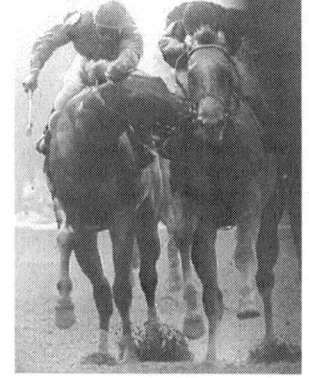

The picture on the left is called 'The Savage.' It was taken in the 1980 Premont Stakes. Great Prospector on the left reaches over and bites Golden Derby as they come down the stretch. Golden Derby eventually wins the race and Great Prospector was second. I will say this is the only horse who did not win and will still be remembered. Horses do not bite each other in racing but Great Prospector was trying hard to find a way to win. He was competing!

WEDNESDAY - "The greatest round of boxing"
Gatti vs Ward - 9th Round

Levi Nile, a journalist for The Bleacher Report, wrote an article about what many believe was the greatest round of boxing ever. Arturo Gatti and Mickey Ward had already absorbed many blows and body punches leading up to the round. Nile's writing is a great way to understand the significance of the fight without being able to show you the actual round here.

As the eighth round ended, Jim Lampley gave voice to what we were all feeling. "Oh my god," he said. "Oh, my goodness! What a fight!"

It's hard to believe that with all the action we had seen to that point, we still had not seen it reach the crescendo. Little did we know we were just one minute away from arguably the greatest round in the televised history of the sport.

For nearly 30 seconds after the knockdown, Ward conducted target practice on Gatti uncontested, firing at will, landing brutally hard hooks to the head and body while getting full extension on his shots. Gatti wasn't rolling with the shots; he was getting knocked around by them like a man in a 10-car pileup. The fact that he managed to absorb so much punishment after such a damaging knockdown is nothing short of unbelievable.

Culture Defeats Strategy 2 - Goonville, Texas Pop. 11

The fact that he was able to mount a comeback after Ward had punched him out, and delivering a full minute of such abuse was the stuff of legend.

"This should be the round of the century!" said Steward as both fighters staggered back to their stools.

And he was exactly right. CompuBox numbers yielded yet another staggering statistic: Gatti had landed 42 of 61 power punches (69 percent), while Ward had landed 60 of 81 (73 percent).

After such an incredible round, the next and final frame passed without much incident; Gatti showed incredible recuperative powers, got back on his bike and used his superior boxing to keep Ward at bay and win the round, thus putting it firmly in the hands of the judges.

The judges awarded the victory to Ward by a narrow decision, but it really didn't matter whom the judges declared as the winner; the fight was so great it transcended the opinions of three men ringside and was destined to be a trilogy.

Baylor's Matt Rhule spoke of showing that round to his team when emphasizing grit and toughness. During the round, the announcers actually said at different times both boxers 'were done' and about to go down.

@CoachJacksonTPW   #culturematters

Culture Defeats Strategy 2 - Goonville, Texas Pop. 11

Coach Rhule said, "When you play football tell your team that your opponent is thinking, 'let's do this and get on with our business.' It's not about how it looks. Football is and always will be a physical game with body blows like both of these boxers took time and time again. We are going to outlast them at Baylor."

Show your team the ninth round, but pause it at times during the round and get a discussion going of what core values they see. Of our values, it's very easy to tie in Compete, Blue Collar Tough (mental toughness as well), Finish and Pay Day.

THURSDAY - '300' Final battle scene

"Long I pondered my King's cryptic talk of victory. Time has proven him wise. For from free Greek to free Greek, the word was spread that bold Leonidas and his 300, so far from home, laid down their lives; not just for Sparta, but for all Greece and the promise this country holds. Now, here on this ragged patch of earth called Plataea, let his hordes face obliteration! Just there the barbarians huddle, sheer terror gripping tight their hearts with icy fingers -- knowing full well what merciless horrors they suffered at the swords and spears of 300. Yet they stare now across the plain at 10,000 Spartans commanding 30,000 free troops. The enemy outnumber us a paltry 3 to 1, good odds for any Greek. This day we rescue a world from mysticism and tyranny and usher in a future brighter than anything we can imagine. Give thanks, men, to Leonidas and the brave 300. TO VICTORY!!!

This is Spartan commander Dilios' 'call to battle' speech before the final scene in the movie '300.'

Culture Defeats Strategy 2 - Goonville, Texas Pop. 11

Although the movie has been out for a few years, most young people will know about the story.

They all want to be a remembered hero. Don't just talk about the heroes that are remembered, show them through clips and they will look forward to the leadership development time with you each day.

CHAPTER 3 REVIEW
THE DAILY FISTFIGHT

- [ ] Even the programs who do a good job of having core values sometimes fail to commit to the daily 'fistfight' of teaching them.

- [ ] A daily leadership development must be a mini-classroom time to have an elite culture.

- [ ] Everyone learns differently but the lowest form of teaching is 'standing and delivering.' When we use this technique, our audience is only retaining about 5% of the message.

- [ ] Direct teachers make sure their students understand the lesson. Be a teacher, not a presenter.

- [ ] Keep your team on edge by using callbacks, walking around, asking questions frequently and getting them up on the board.

- [ ] Coaches must take time to preplan them and use every tool they can to connect with all the students' senses.

- [ ] Our brains are wired to connect with stories. Stories were the 'movie clip' of the past but they are still – and always will be – a must for teachers to use in every lesson.

- [ ] Everyone loves movies. Use short movie clips you can tie into your message.

- [ ] Commit to teaching your culture daily!

CHAPTER 4
LESSON #3 - HELP RAISE THEM

> *"What coaches don't realize is when you're in a huddle with a kid after a timeout or something, you see a look on their face that nobody will ever see. Their parents will never see that look. Their teachers will never see that look. Nobody will ever see that look on a kid's face during a game but us. It's different. The stress, competition, jubilation, sorrow, hurt. All that. Most people never see that in the stands."*
>
> W.T. Johnson
> Head Football Coach
> Newton High School, Newton, Texas

WHO IS YOUR FAVORITE ASSISTANT COACH AND WHY?

"Coach Anderson because he has **treated me like I'm his son**. He is **always there** when I need him. I know he **would do anything for me**."

"Coach Porter because I feel like he **believes in me** and the program unconditionally."

"Coach Luster. The guy is just **awesome**! He goes from 0 to 100 back to 0 in a span of 3 seconds. The guy is just **awesome!**"

"Coach Velasquez! He has been someone **I have looked up** to since the day he got here, all the things I learned from him are things that I will hold onto."

"Coach Wallis is just an **easy guy to talk** to and **super understanding.** I also feel like **I can tell him anything.**"

"Coach Delgado. He **listens to me** and always pushes me to improve daily."

"Coach Granado because he knew when to jump my butt but also knew when we could **joke around and have fun.** I believe if I broke down on the side of the road **he would be there in a heartbeat.**"

"**Practice is fun** because of Coach Luster. He brings the juice every day!"

"Coach Ennis because he held me to a higher standard and kept a close **relationship with me and the defensive line.** He pushed us to be the best unit every day and **loved us at the same time.**"

"Coach Sotak was always there, **listened and was understanding** about situations."

"Coach Ford because he was always **helping me.** He **talked to me** and let me know what to do to help me get better."

"Coach Chancellor, he **keeps me in check**, always makes me better but is **always there for me.**"

Culture Defeats Strategy 2 - Goonville, Texas Pop. 11

THE GOOGLE FORM

Every year within a few days of the end of the season I send the varsity players a Google form with several questions dealing with all aspects of the season.

Examples are: 'What was your favorite core value?'
'On a scale of 1-10 how well do you feel like we emphasized our core values each day?'
'What was the #1 thing you are most proud of from this season?'

One of my favorites each year is **'What did you learn from this program you will take with you that will help you the rest of your life?'**

Answers from this year were:
'Core values.'
'Work ethic and grit.'
'The Process and never looking at the scoreboard.'
'How to work for and earn what I get.'
'You have to be disciplined, focused and give maniacal effort at all times.'
'Because of this program I am inspired to be blue collar in all aspects of my life and be a true goon on and off the field.'

The answers above are actually the first six responses (unedited) from the 2017 season. Answers to this question are always inspiring to me because they primarily describe what the coaching staff teaches daily.

I began the chapter with actual answers from absolutely, positively the most important question on the entire form; **Who was your favorite assistant coach and why?** This is so important to me I warn the staff about it when we begin our preseason meetings in July. I tell them, "if you don't get a vote from at least one player you may not be retained for the next season." We debrief on every aspect of our program when the season is over but nothing is more important than us analyzing the answers from the end of season players' form.

If you truly want to know what your program is about, go to the source. Ask your players with an anonymous survey like a Google form.

THE HEAD COACH IS THE 'DAD' - THE ASSISTANT COACHES ARE THE 'UNCLES'

My big 'aha' from the Google form answers I got the first time a few years ago is that the head coach is responsible for setting the culture and standard. 'Grit, hard work, earn everything' is what we are about. Every year it works out the same way. The life lessons are our core values and the favorite coaches are because they are relational with them.
I reiterate to the players all the time, "I am here to help raise you just like I have helped raise my own two kids. When I yell to my son, 'hey Russ!' He responds with, 'yes sir?' 'Come here,' I say and he immediately comes to the living room and says, 'Sir?' "Guys, he didn't just talk like this on his own. I am lucky he is a good kid, but we helped make him that way. You have my word, myself and this staff are going to help raise you also."

The job of the head coach is to make sure the culture is right. In our case at North Forney, I'm the 'dad' or head of the family. The assistant coaches are the uncles that are still very much part of the family but a little different in a few ways. It's an analogy most of my players understand, or can at least comprehend. It was one thing for your uncle to find out you had done something 'not so good' but for most of us it was better than our dad finding out. Our dad's #1 job was to raise us and he would probably correct the situation more severely so he didn't have to deal with it again.

> *"Winning and championships are memorable but they come from the strength of the relationships."*
>
> **Jim Calhoun**
> **Head Men's Basketball Coach**
> **UConn**

When we look at our players as 'adopted' by us our mindset will be where it needs to be. When we are frustrated by an athlete who is testing our patience (again) if we ask ourselves, 'would I ignore it if it was an actual family member?' We know we couldn't, we would address it again and again because it's our job as his dad, uncle or brother. We would feel that responsibility in our gut to not let it slide.

OUR JOB IS TO HELP 'RAISE THEM UP'

Real parenting is tough. It's a never-ending job we cannot let slide and hope for the best. Coaches with this mindset are heroes our society can't live without. It's not for everyone. When I interview a linebacker coach I'm not only trying to figure out what he can bring to the table on the field, but more importantly will he be one of the few who 'get it', who can truly help us raise our guys off the field. Finding a knowledgeable candidate who can coach linebackers, although it's a little different in each system, is much easier to find than one who has a heart for kids and wants to be 'one of the five.'

> **"If you're afraid of confrontation, you're not going to do very well."**
>
> **Bill Parcells**
> **Former NFL Head Coach**

One way we help raise them is require them to let us know where they are if they aren't present when they are supposed to be with us.

At my house, when my kids were in high school anytime they left they had to tell either me or their mom where they are going and when they expected to be back. If they changed their plans, they texted without fail. We tell our parents it works the same way in our program. We can't say we are going to help them raise them and not care that we don't know where they are.

We are a morning practice team so every now and then one of our guys will be late. When we meet as a team before practice I always get a report in front of the team of who's not accounted for. "DP is not here," our running back coach will say. "Have you heard from him?" I'll ask. "No sir, but I have a text in to him and his parents." Our coaches have a big job that requires a lot of time and energy. When one of their unit players is not present I want to know where he is and if he has communicated. Just like I would want to know where my own two kids, Russ or Katie, are if I haven't heard from them. If the athlete hasn't communicated then I am asking our coach if he has reached out to the parent(s). The parents are either appreciative we care this much or irritated we are pestering them early in the morning. Either way they need to be aware their son is not where he is supposed to be. In the rare instance, he has had car trouble or an accident, we all need to know.

> *"If you love them, you're going to discipline them. If you don't love them, you're going to let them do whatever they want."*
>
> **Mark Richt**
> **Retired SEC Football Coach**

THE CRITICAL DECADE - OUR RELATIONSHIP WITH THEM COULD BE THE MOST IMPACTFUL

We all know the 'typical family' stats aren't good but let's look at today's home life. Our teams are full of players with a dad barely raising them or not raising them at all.
- 40% have no dad at home.
- 40% have a distracted dad who travels too much, etc.
- 20% have a 'normal dad' who is home most of the time.

In 2001, the federal government unveiled a new education initiative called 'No Child Left Behind.' One thing the unpopular program did (it was repealed in 2015) was figure out the average 10-year span of human development.   They called it the critical decade and for most of us it's between the ages of 15-25. At age 25, the average person is getting married and starting the cycle all over again by having kids of their own.

What did they say was the #1 factor that led to 'normal' adults, those who had made it out of the critical decade? They had - on average - FIVE adults they felt cared about them, were there for them, and had their best interest at heart.

Think about this. If you have children how many do they have? Will they have a total of five during the critical decade? My daughter, Katie, didn't participate in any sports so I've often wondered if she will have five adults she knows cares about her and pours into her on a regular basis. Russ wrestled at Grapevine High School so he was around three wrestling coaches who I know, and he knows, cared about him. Both are good kids and have a bright future but Russ definitely had more adults who will have helped him get through the critical decade.

RELATIONSHIPS MATTER FOR MAXIMUM PERFORMANCE

In the article, 'Relationships Matter' by Deborah Stipek, she explains how important relationships are to academic performance by students of all ages. *Young children share their feelings and information about themselves with teachers who are affectionate and nurturing. These close relationships with teachers lead to higher levels of student engagement and achievement. When young children are asked how they know their teachers care about them, they refer to them being attentive. 'She says 'hi' to me when I come in the room.'*

'She saves a snack for me at snack time,' and *'She makes sure I get a turn.'*

These are all non-academic needs being met that are building personal relationships that will enhance performance.

Stipek also says adolescents are no different than the younger children. *They report that they work harder for teachers who treat them as individuals and express interest in their personal lives outside school. Caring teachers, they report, are also honest, fair, and trusting.*

Personal relationships with the at-risk student is even more important. *When researchers ask youths who have dropped out of high school why they left school, the young people frequently say it was because no one cared.* **Those who stay in school cite meaningful relationships with adults who show an interest in them as individuals** *(National Research Council, 2004). In a 1997 Public Agenda phone survey, 64 percent of students claimed that they would learn more if their teachers* **"personally cared about their students as people;"** *unfortunately, only 30 percent claimed that most of their teachers did care. According to a recent large survey of high school students, African American students were particularly responsive to teachers who showed that they cared about the students' learning (Ferguson, 2002). When asked why they worked hard when they did, 47 percent checked, "My teachers encourage me to work hard;" only* **15 percent checked, "My teacher demanded it."**

Culture Defeats Strategy 2 - Goonville, Texas Pop. 11

> *"Regard your soldiers as your children, and they will follow you into the deepest valleys; look on them as your own beloved sons, and they will stand by you even unto death."*
>
> Sun Tzu

"If I have a player who comes from a poor home environment and I just buy him a candy bar he will be loyal to me for a week," Winnsboro, Texas head coach Josh Finney told me. "It's one thing to tell a kid you care about him but it's nothing like giving him a dollar for a snack." Josh and I have coached together at a couple of schools and he is one of the best at meeting them where they need it. I know we can't feed every kid every day but when we do help them it's really making the 'I am going to help raise you' culture meaningful.

Dusti Douglas, a college classmate and friend, has been a middle school math teacher for over 20 years. She gets results and has very few discipline problems because in her own words, "I momma them and don't take no for an answer. When I have a student missing work, I go find him or her at lunch and tell them to bring their food to my room so we can get their assignment finished. They sometimes act perturbed but they know I care about them and it makes all the difference. They call me 'Momma Douglas' because I'll go hunt them down and make sure we get it done." Dusti is helping raise them like a parent who won't allow failure by laziness. It takes a lot of effort to do it this way but it is almost fail-proof.

Bo Hanson, writer for Athlete Assessment website, wrote The Coach Athlete Relationship is a Performance Factor. In it he writes, *Coaches are known as an athlete's **primary caregiver**. They are the people in the* athletes lives who are expected to provide security, safety, and emotional support. *The fact is, we as human beings are conditioned to wanting this from our coaches as a result of how we have been parented in our early childhood years.* Hanson later states if an athlete is made to feel secure (just like if an elementary teacher saves a snack for her student) they are more likely to attempt new techniques, push their boundaries, and give 100% effort. *It's no wonder the coach-athlete relationship is a performance factor that extends beyond all others. It is literally hardwired into us from our very first hours of being born,* Hanson writes.

Another study of the coach-athlete relationship was conducted by Penny Wurthner on the 2008 Canadian Olympic team. She concluded there are five significant factors for all the athletes who either won a medal or set a personal best at the games.

The Five Factors for Success

1. <u>The Coach-Athlete Relationship</u> - Mutual trust, predictability, and communication between each other.
2. <u>Athlete Self-Awareness</u> - their mental training, what motivates them, and how they adapt their behavior to succeed.

3. <u>Quality of the Training Environment</u> - equipment, strength and conditioning training, and overall facilities.

4. <u>Management of Competitive Environment</u> - how well the logistics were managed so as to not limit the athlete's training and performance.

5. <u>Support Environment</u> - people in the athlete's lives. Family, friends, doctors, nutritionists, trainers, etc.

The most significant contributor to an outstanding performance by the Olympians was a meaningful and productive coach-athlete relationship. As always, everything mattered for the Olympians but what mattered most was the relationship he/she had with her coach.

What do other coaches want from someone coaching **their child? They want someone who they trust to take care of him or her.** In a ESPN college football poll, they asked FBS coaches if they had a son playing college football, and were no longer coaching, which current FBS coach would you want him to play for? Former Miami coach Mark Richt and ex-OU coach Bob Stoops tied as the #1 choice. Next were ex-Minnesota coach Jerry Kill, Stanford's David Shaw and Duke's David Cutcliffe.

CBS sports did the same poll for Division 1 basketball coaches and Michigan State head man Tom Izzo received the most votes. Said one coach, "Tom Izzo might be the most likable big-time coach we have. Great coach and great guy. I'd let my sons play for him any day. You won't find many people -- maybe not *any* people -- who don't respect Coach Izzo."

> *"The old lessons (work, self-discipline, sacrifice, teamwork, fighting to achieve) aren't being taught by many people other than football coaches these days. The football coach has a captive audience and can teach these lessons because the communication lines between himself and his players are more wide open than between kids and parents."*
>
> Bear Bryant

RELATIONSHIPS ARE ABOUT 1-on-1 COMMUNICATION

During the 2017 season at North Forney we were fortunate to have Tate Wallis on our staff to coach the receivers and help with the offense. Tate coached at Baylor for eight years so he was able to learn not only how to score points in bunches, but he also got a front row seat on how to develop relationships and communicate with players one-on-one. Tate was one of our most relational coaches. He built individual rapport with each of our receivers that was invaluable to them individually and us as a team. We had an extremely talented receiving corps, but as you can surmise from Chapter 1, they needed to grow with the rest of the team in discipline, accountability and work ethic. Many of them had a chance to continue playing at the collegiate level but they needed a wakeup call on what it would take. Coach Wallis had instant credibility, our guys knew he was 'real' when he talked to them about how D1 receivers work.

One of my go-to questions I ask college coaches when they come through NF is, "What is the #1 thing your program does to develop relationships with players?" It was fairly quickly after Tate arrived when I asked him the same question. He thought for a second and said, "Coach Briles told us to spend the time necessary to have real conversations. That was one of his beliefs, to take the time to stop, look them in the eye, and find out how they are really doing. Never to just say, 'how's it going?' and keep walking."

Tate and I together formed the quintessential 'I'm the dad and he is the uncle' tandem. When I would "go off" for lack of a better term on the entire team or an individual player about effort, discipline, toughness or anything we were trying desperately to instill, Tate would walk to them later and whisper in their ear. I never knew exactly what it was he was saying to them but it was meaningful and each receiver matured as a player and person under his tutelage. Most of them did sign to play at the next level. Because of Coach Wallis they have a much greater chance to make it and be big time contributors.

It's amazing how impactful one-on-one conversations can be with people. If you played any sport, try and think back to one of your coaches who took just a short time to talk to you about anything other than your sport. It's tough for me to recall as I'm sure it is for many of you. Just like being intentional with a daily plan for leadership development, we must have a plan or system to spend a few meaningful moments with our athletes one-on-one.

Meaningful conversation with your own kids are tough to have and most of our players are not getting much of it at home.

Culture Defeats Strategy 2 - Goonville, Texas Pop. 11

In the book, 'Leaders Eat Last', author Simon Sinek describes how coach Gregg Popovich of the San Antonio Spurs has a routine to connect with his players at the beginning of each practice. He enters the gym wearing a t-shirt, cargo shorts, and flip flops. His hair is uncombed and he has a large coffee in one hand. Although he doesn't look much like one of the greatest basketball coaches ever, this is when he does some of his best work. This is when he goes around to each player as they are doing their pre-practice shooting. 'Pop' walks up to them one at a time, gently grabs them by the elbow and speaks to them about things other than basketball. "Coach fills everyone's cup individually", writes Sinek.

When Lou Holtz coached at Notre Dame his recruiting coordinator made a video to send to potential recruits. Holtz loved everything about it but thought it would help sell the program a little more if a few clips of Holtz having positive interactions with players were added. A few days later the recruiting coordinator informed Coach Holtz he tried but couldn't find any. This took Holtz by surprise because he thought he was a positive coach. "I became more aware of my 1-on-1 interactions with players after this. It was humbling and I needed the wake-up call," said Holtz.

My son, Russ, did not play football after ninth grade. He decided he wasn't in love with it but he had a passion for wrestling. I was fine with his decision because I wanted him to only do something he couldn't live without, and I believed in our wrestling coach, Kent Hall. Coach Hall would hold him accountable but still be patient and help him love the game. Coach Hall would be 'one of the five' Russ needed.

@CoachJacksonTPW #culturematters

Culture Defeats Strategy 2 - Goonville, Texas Pop. 11

After a year, Coach Hall resigned from coaching to pursue another opportunity in our school district. As the campus coordinator, I had a say in who the next head wrestling coach would be. As we interviewed the candidates what do you think concerned me the most? Correct, it wasn't all about wrestling knowledge. I had to make sure we found a great teacher, wrestling coach, and mentor for my son and all wrestlers at Grapevine High School. We hired Matt Criner and I could not be more pleased with the three years Russ spent with him.

Even after graduation Russ has continued to compete. He no longer wrestles but 'rolls' in Jiu Jitsu. I asked him about his coach, Jason Sampson, and he said, "He pulls me aside quite a bit and tells me how good he thinks I will be one day. He makes me feel like he believes in me. No matter what I have to do I'm not going to let him down." It's easy for me to tell how Russ talks about Coach Sampson. He would lay in traffic for him. We all need to feel like someone believes in us. I'm grateful my son still has this in his life even after he's finished with high school sports.

I sit in a hallway outside the locker room each morning before and after practice or workout. Before workout we have the 'core value song of the day' going and I'm sitting in a spot to catch everyone, to 'relate and motivate' early in the morning. It's mostly about encouraging and letting them know how fired up I am to coach them that day.

After practice, I'm in the same spot but my mission is different. Everyone is in a good mood when the work is done, so this is the time to 'look them in the eye' and engage them individually. Some days I do better than

Culture Defeats Strategy 2 - Goonville, Texas Pop. 11

others, but this is my intentional time to connect with our players.

"Cam, I want you to know how much we appreciate you and don't take you for granted," I said to senior offensive lineman Cam Rogers. Cam is one of those steady, very good players who punches the time clock every day. If we aren't careful, we'll spend all our time on the 3-5% who are 'high maintenance' and forget to thank our players who we love to coach. "Thanks coach, that means a lot to me," Cam replied. It was easy to tell from the look on his face he meant it. What a great job we have.

> **"Appreciation is the currency of success."**
>
> **Shaka Smart**
> **Head Basketball Coach**
> **University of Texas**

Brian Cain, my mental coach and mentor, has helped me take it to another level with 1 on 1 conversations with players. "Each day you must find 5 minutes to have a 1 on 1 time with an athlete. After practice walk around the track and talk about anything other than football."

THEY WILL 'LAY IN TRAFFIC' FOR COACHES THEY LOVE

I have yet to get a favorite coach response from our Google form after the season that says, "He taught me to post inside and cut off penetration on my pass set," or "Coach Smith was the best rugby tackling coach I have ever had. Because of him I felt safer than ever."

The responses are always about relationships. Teenagers want to be heard, they want to share their dreams with us. Although it's oftentimes through social media, they are constantly telling their story. To be 'one of the five' for any young person we are blessed enough to coach we must remember our role is just the vehicle that allows us to be around them for hours each day. Just because we're their coach doesn't mean we're filling their cup and helping raise them.

Back to the Google form. I bolded all the significant parts of each response that related to relationships: 'he treated me like his son' - 'would do anything for me' - 'listened to me' - 'easy to talk to' - 'could tell him anything' - 'would come help me in a heartbeat' - 'loved us.'

FOOD CONNECTS US

Another way we also do to make it a program they can't live without is to understand relationships are built away from the facility. I tell my guys they must find a way to do something off campus at times. Sharing meals together is the #1 way for us. Our state governing body, the University Interscholastic League, has deemed food is legal to provide for players, so we are going to eat with them. Food brings people together. Think about every family gathering you have been to since you were a child. There's always a good meal involved if it's a joyous occasion in the least.

The Spartans believed the 'common mess' was a great tactic to bind troops together. Even married troops were required to eat with their platoon in the mess until they were 30 years old. Above the threshold of each mess was a sign that said: **Out this door, nothing.**

"Even horses and dogs who are fed together," observed Spartan commander Xenophon, "form bonds and become attached to one another."

The summer before the 2017 (and each summer thereafter) season, I invited groups of 7-8 players to eat lunch with me and an assistant coach at a local restaurant. I knew this would be a great way to have some time to talk about each other and what it would take to get this program headed in the right direction. After we got our food I asked them a few questions to loosen them up and get them talking.

- 'What's your favorite TV show or movie?'

- 'What's your favorite subject and who's your favorite teacher?'

- 'What's one of your main goals for this season?'

I also opened up about me and my situation. Although I had been at NF for a few months it had been '100 mph' since day one. I asked them questions like, "Do you know where I grew up? Where I go to church? I had told them this before but most did not know much about my personal life. Me and the coach with me shared some of our personal history with them; where we went to high school, college and a little bit about our families.

We then discussed a book I had recently read titled 'The Captain Class,' by Sam Walker. This is an excellent book that describes what the most dominant professional sports dynasties had in common – elite captains. The captains were not usually the most talented player on the team, but they were the true leaders. Most of the captains were servant leaders or the 'water carriers.' I told each group I ate with that summer, "if we're going to be special this season, it'll be because we have more servant leaders than our opponents. Every team we play will have tremendous talent, but we must out-captain them to shock the state and make a playoff run."

Handshakes

If you have not seen the video of Wake Forest football player, Cortez Lewis, do yourself a favor and YouTube it. Lewis has over 50 different handshakes for 50 different teammates. Andrea Adelson of ESPN.com chronicled Lewis' handshake rituals. *Lewis says he has handshakes with students in his classes and basketball players, too. All told, he has no idea how many handshakes he actually has with people. "Maybe 70?" he says. "It's over 50."*

Losing track doesn't really seem that out of the ordinary, considering how many people are in his loop. What is extraordinary is that A, each handshake is unique; and B, he remembers every single handshake, its moves coming to mind as soon as he sees the person's face. Lewis says the ritual started in high school. "That's how I kept up with people. I had handshakes so I always kept up good relationships with people."

I'm not the smartest guy in the world but if Lewis and I had a personal handshake I would be fired up every time I saw him approaching. I have three guys (all defensive linemen who I'm not around as much) I have personalized handshakes with. This season each position coach came up with a handshake for his guys. Of course, they loved it.

As I was writing this book I asked our 'Goonville Council' (what we call our booster club) if anyone had a good story they would share about a relationship their son formed with a coach from the 2017 season.

Below is one of the few stories I received. It is from Suzi Rodriguez talking about her son, Carlos, and his relationship with Zach Geer, our kicking coach and head baseball coach at the time.

*"This may not be exactly what you're looking for, because it's not a specific thing. My son changed a lot when he found that **someone was paying attention**. Prior to you taking over, Carlos never felt like he knew who he should go to, who his leader was or who could help him. Now, he has Coach Geer's cell number, email, whatever he needs to get in touch with him. **He pays attention, he holds him accountable, and shows up and cares about where he is and what he's doing.** It's made an enormously positive impact on my son."*

CHAPTER 4 REVIEW
HELP RAISE THEM

- Favorite coaches are favorites because they're relational on a deep level.

- Use a Google form to survey your team and get feedback about where your coaches are on the '1 of the 5' scale.

- If we view them as our children we're trying to help raise it will give us the correct lens to look through while coaching them.

- Hold them accountable but love them through it. Be a 'daddy' or 'momma.' They may fuss but they want us to make them succeed.

- Food is a great conduit for relationships. The most meaningful way to connect with your players is away from the facility.

CHAPTER 5
LESSON #4 - LEADERS EAT LAST

> *"The cost of leadership is self-interest."*
>
> **George Flynn**
> **U.S. Army General**

COURTLAND SUTTON SWEEPING THE SHED

Each year coach Chad Morris, the former head coach at SMU, and his staff begin fall camp with 'The Big Weigh In.' It's a high-energy event where they weigh each athlete and compare his weight, strength, and speed improvements over the summer and celebrate all improvements hard. We wanted to do this at NF so I asked if a couple of coaches and I could attend in 2017, their last year at SMU. Coach Morris is an ex-high school coach, so he 'gets it,' and is always uber hospitable when they are practicing.

The 'Big Weigh-In' was held in the team meeting room and it was packed. It was an hour plus of juice, celebration, high fives and proud Mustangs. When it was over, the team was released to their 'welcome back' meal of ribeye steak. As we were thanking Coach Morris and others for allowing us to invade their first meeting of the season, I noticed a couple of players taking extra chairs that had been put in the back for capacity seating back to unit meeting rooms. Having spent some time at SMU I quickly realized one of them was All-American receiver Courtland Sutton.

Courtland was the undisputed alpha player on the team who could have left early and declared for the NFL draft. Instead, he returned for his redshirt junior season, had another great year and was drafted early in the second round the next spring by the Denver Broncos.

Sutton wasn't worried about getting in line early to eat. He was serving by putting up chairs in a room where very few people remained to see him do it. I took this picture knowing he might think it was a little odd but it was such a teachable moment I had to have a visual to share with our team. Sutton was like the All-Black rugby captains sweeping the shed and it was awesome to witness firsthand. I don't know what the future holds for him in the NFL, but I do know he will make their team better with his character and servant leadership.

USMC MESS HALL 'CODE'

Simon Sinek wrote the best-selling book, 'Leaders Eat Last,' in 2014. When Sinek was doing research, he interviewed USMC General George Flynn and asked him what makes the Marines' leadership style so dominant.

"Leaders eat last," was Flynn's quick reply. "This fundamental concept explains what makes the USMC so extraordinarily tight-knit, to the point that they willingly trust their lives to one another. In every chow hall across the globe, Marines line up for their food each day, and the most junior ranking Marines eat first. Their leaders eat last. It's not in any handbook or procedural manual. It's just the way Marine leadership teaches responsibility," said Flynn.

I hadn't thought about this concept before reading 'Leaders Eat Last' and made the mistake of letting the seniors eat first at our team dinners. I think about it differently now. For the Marines, true leadership is the willingness to place others' needs above your own. Being a senior is not a privilege, but a responsibility.

LEADERS SERVE THE TEAM

In Chapter 4, I mentioned going over the book, 'The Captain Class,' by Sam Walker, with our team in the summer of 2017. This is a book all leaders should read and a concept all need to introduce to their programs. Our core value of family encompasses many things we teach, but servant leadership is at the top.

What you celebrate you get more of. To celebrate your servant leaders, you must first find out who they are. Our motto last year was 'Brick by Brick.' I decided to foster the

Culture Defeats Strategy 2 - Goonville, Texas Pop. 11

'this team will create the foundation' mindset. Each player got a brick the first day of fall camp and wrote their name, number, and favorite core value on it. Every so often we would get the bricks out and write something else like, 'why do you play football?' 'who is the most influential person in your life?' or 'who on the team would you most want in a time of war to get in a foxhole with?'

We elect captains before district play starts, so, to reemphasize how important our servant leaders are to the team, I got a clean brick and told the team, "I want everyone to pass this brick around and write the name of the #1 servant leader on our team. The one guy who you know would be there for you if your car was broken down. The guy who sweeps the shed so the group doesn't bear-crawl for a locker room not up to our standard. The one guy who would carry the water for the team and not mind doing it." It was awesome to see the different names on the brick. Connor Sides, a senior reserve receiver, had his name on the brick the most times. Connor was a true servant leader for us. He was also elected one of our six captains a few days later.

Recently I visited the BSN headquarters in Addison, Texas. While touring the facility one of the managers told me the company was approached by a major sports apparel brand to gauge their interest in helping with a campaign that celebrates the "look at me" culture we have in sports now. They were interested in an ad campaign that would focus on kids playing sports and self-promoting after making a great play. BSN said, "thanks but no thanks, this is not something our company stands for." Thank you, BSN. Our job is tough enough in the world we live in now without celebrating the individual.

Two Post-Practice Cultures

In 2010, when Dez Bryant was a rookie, he and fellow receiver Roy Williams got into a verbal altercation when Dez refused to carry the veteran's pads in after a practice. The 'tradition' for the Cowboys and other NFL teams was (and might still be) that rookies had to carry in pads after each session when they were in Thousand Oaks for training camp practices. Dez decided this was disrespectful (probably threw up his 'X') and began to walk in the locker room.

"I'm not doing it," Bryant said. "I feel like I was drafted to play football, not carry another player's pads. If I was a free agent, it would still be the same thing. I just feel like I'm here to play football. I'm here to try to help win a championship, not carry someone's pads. I'm saying that out of no disrespect to [anyone]."

Veteran player Roy Williams believed it was something everyone needed to do. "Everybody has to go through it," he said. "I had to go through it. No matter if you're a No. 1 pick or the 7,000th pick, you've still got to do something when you're a rookie".

"I carried pads. I paid for dinners. I paid for lunches. I did everything I was supposed to do, because I didn't want to be that guy."

Pads were also getting carried off the field after practices in Tampa Bay for many seasons. But, the intent and therefore the culture is a little different. Gerald McCoy, an All-Pro former defensive tackle for the Buccaneers, started carrying pads when he went in years ago. He didn't care whose pads they were, it could be rookies, free agents, whoever was in camp with him.

"You have to serve before you can lead," McCoy said. "That's what I was always taught and that's what I believe in. If you give everything you have, some days you don't have anything left. Anything I can do to help the man next to me to propel themselves to being better, I will do."

I'm sure we can all agree which culture would be the most beneficial for a great team chemistry. We used the video of McCoy carrying in the pads in one of our Leadership Academy lessons. I hadn't seen the 'Hard Knocks' episode where it originated, but one of our players spoke up and said, McCoy was actually so worried about taking care of others he forgot his own helmet.

Find stars like Courtland Sutton and Gerald McCoy and show your team what true servant leaders look like and some of them will decide to serve others as well. It only takes a couple to grab a pad and others will follow.

> *"The servant-leader is a servant first. It begins with the natural feeling that one wants to serve, to serve first."*
>
> Robert K. Greenleaf

THERE'S A LOT MORE TO COACHING THAN PUTTING ON THE WHISTLE

In 1989, I did my student-teaching at Calhoun Middle School in Calhoun, Louisiana. My supervising teacher was Steve Reid, who was the campus coordinator and head football coach. Coach Reid was a 20+ year veteran so I was extremely fortunate to get to learn under him. I grew up in a coaching and teaching household, my father Raymond, coached for 41 years in Texas so I was eager to start my career and probably felt like I was more ready than I actually was.

I played tight end, but we worked with the offensive line a lot of the time so I was 100% ready to go coach me some OL! I knew I could get them to do the 'little things' coach J.B. Grimes taught us (now the OL coach at Auburn). We would work daily on taking a six-inch step and then get their second step down quickly, shoot our hands, and drive with a wide base. I would be intense, demanding, and we would work quickly. My attitude was 'just give me a month with those 7th graders and everyone in NE Louisiana will be amazed by our skill.' It would be elephants on parade, a symphony of down blocks and zone steps.

The first day of practice was like Christmas in early August for me. I had my whistle, CMS cap and shirt, and was ready to go make it happen. After all, I was

Culture Defeats Strategy 2 - Goonville, Texas Pop. 11

exposed to some great coaching at NLU (now Louisiana Monroe) for the last four years and was ready to go help these little guys love playing football.

"Coach Jackson, you stay up in the locker room for a few minutes when we start our stretch to help the late ones figure out how to put their pads in their pants," Coach Reid said to me. "Yes, sir," I responded. Every coach probably remembers the first they were ever called "Coach." It was awesome.

Put their pads in their pants? They really don't know how to do this? I was sure he was just being cautious. I started playing full pad football in 3rd grade and couldn't remember not knowing how to put knee pads in. As usual, the veteran coach was right, and most of the late guys didn't know.

"Coach Jackson, at water break I need you to go stand by the water hose and make sure they don't spray each other. Tell them to get a drink and not horse around," Coach Reid told me. Ok, he was right about them not knowing how to put knee pads in but there is NO WAY they would squirt water on each other. This is 'school' football, not little league.

"Don't do that," I said within about a minute. One of the guys was squirting another one with water. "Stick and move. Don't waste time when time is involved" (at least I could use those terms I learned from Coach Pat Collins at NLU).

"How was your first practice, Randy?" Coach Reid asked me later. "It was good, but I have to admit it was a little more like youth football than I was expecting." (I chuckle even typing this). It was

@CoachJacksonTPW #culturematters

Culture Defeats Strategy 2 - Goonville, Texas Pop. 11

nothing like I was expecting. I didn't remember coaches monitoring the water hose when I played in elementary.

Coach Reid was about to drop some real wisdom with his next statement to me. "Never forget this, the easiest part of coaching is putting the whistle around your neck."

What? There is no way this could be true. I have seen elite coaches the last four years coach their butts off. I knew Coach Reid was a veteran with a great reputation but he had to be off on this.

He was 100% on the money.

The easiest part of coaching is when you get to do the actual coaching. The real work is dealing with paperwork, parents, equipment issue, physicals, bus certification, classroom teaching ... I could go on and on.

Another great story from my student teaching experience was being allowed to coach the 7th grade 'B' basketball team. After going through the football season, I knew they would not be as prepared as I thought so I did a better job of coaching what I thought was the obvious.

During the first game, I decided to substitute one of our players in the middle of the first quarter. "Jimmy, go in for Casey," I said to a wide-eyed youngster who might not have ever even seen a game in person before. As soon as the words came out of my mouth, Jimmy ran onto the floor. What?? What the heck? He really didn't know to check in at the scorer's table?

@CoachJacksonTPW   #culturematters

This was my first on-the-job training to understanding Coach Reid's comment. If blowing the whistle is on one end of the spectrum then serving them is on the other.

COACHES MUST ALSO MODEL SERVANT LEADERSHIP

The idea of servant leadership is that the typical hierarchy of the 'boss-employee' relationship is turned upside down. Instead of the employees serving the leaders, the leaders serve the people in their charge. There are several ways coaching staffs can show servant leadership as well in this same paradigm.

The most important part of coaching is helping raise them and serve them.

As I mentioned earlier in the book, I interview to hire coaches who have a heart for kids. At NF, we are going to serve our players in several ways. If you want your seniors to 'eat last,' then you have to model it for them.

Each day we have three coaches assigned to do laundry for our players' workout and game gear. Each player has a strap with a connector to strap their workout gear on. They turn it in after our morning workout and it is washed and put in their laundry locker in our hallway before we go home for the day. Not only is this a way for us to look like a team and help limit staph infections, but it is us serving them. We also wash towels and put them out each day.

Culture Defeats Strategy 2 - Goonville, Texas Pop. 11

Like most staffs, we will pick up players who need a ride before practice or give them a ride home when they need it. We make sure the video is ready online for them to watch practice or opponent film. Our coaches will tutor players after school and even do community service projects with them during the offseason.

But, the biggest thing we do for our players is have a heart for kids. To coach at NF you must have a desire to serve and help our players. We all get busy and are in a hurry to do a million things, but when our players are around we are intentional about being available to them.

A then-retired legendary Texas high school football coach, Steve Lineweaver, once spoke to my staff at Grapevine. One of his biggest points was being patient when a player needs you before or after practice. "The most important coach on any staff is the middle school coach who takes the time to really listen to the seventh-grader who needs him before practice. Imagine the damage done to the psyche of a young man who hasn't ever played, and is scared to death. He needs a coach to answer a question and gets, 'I don't have time for you, get dressed and hurry up!'

Coach Lineweaver added, "I know we are all busy trying to get everything ready for practice, but remember you have the future of the program and a kid's heart in front of you. Take a few seconds to deal with him like you would want your son dealt with."

There is so much wisdom in Coach Lineweaver's message. We all lose players who quit playing for one reason or another, but the way we speak to them shouldn't be one of the reasons they don't continue on.

Another way we serve is to help our guys in the recruiting process. Ben Rudolph coached at NF for two seasons (2017-18) and was one of our guys who 'got it' and was all about the players.

Coach Rudolph is one of those coaches who is always finding ways to pour into others. He was one of our physical education teachers at NF. One of his classes was an adaptive class where the participants were special needs students. Ben was great with them, he was patient and made sure they had fun each day. In the spring, when the time came for the class to get ready for Special Olympics, he went above and beyond for them. He practiced with them days in advance in all their events so they would feel comfortable on 'game day.' He also made sure our team had a part in the Olympics as well. He organized our guys to volunteer and made sure they were serving and encouraging participants during the day.

Another way Ben made members of the P.E. class feel special was by allowing three of them to put out laundry each day. He showed them how to match the numbers from the strap with the locker so they could distribute workout gear for the next morning. Near the end of the school year, Ben asked me if we could take a team pic and have a celebration for the three students who helped the team daily. He had our guys make a tunnel to 'high-five' them as they walked into our indoor facility, and we all took a picture with them. This is one of those special things that validate his P.E.

students, but also showed our players the importance of thanking those who help them.

In the summer of 2018, Ben and his family were traveling back from Florida after a vacation. When they were traveling through Monroe, La., Ben knew he would have a chance to stop and see Colby Suits, our quarterback from the 2017 season. Colby signed a scholarship to play at my old school Louisiana Monroe and was in Monroe for the summer, attending classes and getting ready for the season. Ben and his family took the time to see how one of our former players was doing and take him a Gatorade and a 'Pay Day' bar (one of our core values).

Find coaches for your staff who are more about watching film and model servant leadership like Ben Rudolph did for us. If you do, you will have a culture of service in your program that will be change kids forever.

Unselfishness Leads to Loyalty

Alexander the Great and his army conquered so much territory they literally 'marched off the map' in 330 B.C. When they took land past the Himalayas, his generals came to him saying, "We have marched to unknown land. Our maps are now worthless. We should turn back." Alexander knew he had the greatest army in the world and was not about to stop their momentum. "Great armies march off the map!" he responded.

As they kept moving forward, the land became more and more arid. Water was scarce and Alexander came to a point where he had to make a decision – to keep going or turn back. He sent out scouts to find water as the rest of his troops continued eastward.

Finally, after a few days a detachment of scouts came galloping back to the king. They had found a small spring miles away, but had filled up a helmet with water to give Alexander. As he took the helmet, the entire army was watching to see him take pleasure in some much-needed water.

Alexander thanked the scouts for bringing him this gift, then, without touching a drop, he lifted the helmet and poured every ounce of it onto the dry ground. Instantly, a thunderous cheer roared throughout the columns of troops. "With a king like this to lead us, no force on earth can stand against us," one man was heard to say.

Leave It Better Than We Found It

Another way we can model servant leadership is by making sure the locker room we are using when playing on the road is clean when we leave.

Win or lose, we are going to 'police' the locker room we were allowed to use. Coaches should take the lead in this and not just have the players do it. Like everyone, we have coaches taking care of a million things after a game, but our coaches who are in the locker room will always make sure it is spotless when we leave.

Maybe the best story to come out of the 2018 World Cup was how Japan reacted after a loss that knocked them out of the tournament. After being up 2-0 (a big lead in soccer), the Japanese team allowed Belgium to make a comeback and were defeated, 3-2. The loss wasn't a 'ho-hum' one, but a last-minute heartbreaker in the 94th minute.

After the game, the Japanese players bowed to their fans to thank them for coming to Russia and support them, then not only cleaned the locker room, but left a note in Russian that said, 'thank you.' #classandgrace

*Side note - the Japanese fans stayed and cleaned the stadium after the game as well!

CARRY YOUR SHIELD

Our 2018 motto was 'Carry Your Shield,' based on the Spartan battle tactic of protecting the 'blind spot' of the man to their left with their shield.

The Spartan shields were made out of layers of wood glued together and then a fine layer of bronze covered the surface. The Spartan battle formation was very intimidating when the golden shields glistened off the sun and shone towards the enemy.

The Spartan battle formation was very similar to other ancient armies, they relied on the phalanx. The phalanx was a very tight, rectangular mass of soldiers who relied on everyone pushing their shields against the enemy in

unison. The concept of the shields was so important, commanders would arrange so that family members or friends would be put next to each other within the formation. The thinking was that they would stand and fight that much fiercer for someone they deeply cared about, and less likely to abandon their place in formation when the intense fighting began.

Spartan law also valued the shield. If a warrior lost his helmet or breast plate he would be fined (those were carried for protection of him only), but if he lost his shield, it was punishable by death. The shield protected every man in the line.

Sparta's enemies, when facing the 'wall of bronze' bearing down on them, knew if the phalanx stayed intact, they were in trouble. If the formation did fall apart, the Spartans were left vulnerable. If any soldier was tempted to abandon their shield to flee, they knew it would be too shameful to bear. One famous quote from a Spartan mom when her son was leaving for battle was, "return with your shield, or on it."

I love mottos that have a physical component to them. Something tangible we can give our players and put up on walls. Our guys can see literal shields all over our facility to remind them to protect their family at all cost this season. If we live the 'shield code,' we have a chance to stick together and be special because we will have the strength of the phalanx. If we abandon our shield and play as individuals, we will be like all other teams that sometimes survive ... and sometimes don't.

LEADERS TAKE CARE OF THE FAMILY

1. The Head of the Family is a Protector

Aesop was a Greek philosopher and storyteller who died in 564 B.C. Aesop's fable 'The Four Oxen and the Lion,' tells of the importance of needing a leader who will unify the group.

A Lion used to prowl about a field in which Four Oxen used to dwell.

Many a time he tried to attack them; but whenever he came near they turned their tails to one another, so that whichever way he approached them he was met by the horns of one of them.

At last, however, they fell a-quarrelling among themselves, and each went off to pasture alone in a separate corner of the field.

Then the Lion attacked them one by one and soon made an end of all four.

This fable is from the 6th century and it is still relevant to remind us we cannot work alone. There is strength in numbers, but without an 'alpha' to organize us we will not be a Spartan phalanx.

A true leader protects his family against the 'lions at the door.' He makes everyone around him feel safer with his presence, and bonds the group together.

Culture Defeats Strategy 2 - Goonville, Texas Pop. 11

In 2011, current Boston Celtic Marcus Smart was a high school basketball player at Flower Mound Marcus High School in Flower Mound, Texas. Before a playoff game, they were waiting in the tunnel to take the court when the opposing team began to taunt them. Marcus calmly walked over to the group, stood very close to them and stared them down without saying a word. The taunting stopped, Smart sent a message to both teams he would be the alpha male that night. Marcus High School won the game behind a leader we all would want to play with and coach.

Late in the 2017 season, we were playing at home vs. West Mesquite. They began mocking us with a rhythmic chant of, 'Goonville! Goonville! Goonville!" over and over before the game. This is a chant our own student section came up with early in the fall and was not the first time we had heard it from across the field, but it was the first time another team had actually done it. West was a team NF had never beaten and the margin of victory was always lopsided.

I looked around to see if I could get a sense if it was affecting us at all. Our guys were affected alright. It was pissing us off and I was grateful. "Let's go guys, we will do our talking with this," one said pointing at his helmet. "We've been hearing them talk for years. It's time for us to shut them up," another said.

We ran back the opening kickoff which made me feel even more confident we would not be intimated. We were a team with resolve that had leaders who were protectors. West was a very talented team with several D1 recruits. The game was nip and tuck most of the way until we finally wore them down with our tempo in the fourth quarter. When the smoke cleared we came out

@CoachJacksonTPW   #culturematters

Culture Defeats Strategy 2 - Goonville, Texas Pop. 11

on top, 50-44, and another milestone had been established in Goonville.

2. The Head of the Family has Empathy

Empathy - the ability to understand and share the feelings of others.

The family needs to be a safe place emotionally. A circle of safety not just physically but mentally. A place where we can put ourselves in the shoes of others.

When my kids were smaller I told them, "Outside these walls the world is a mean place. There will be lots of people you meet who do not want you to succeed and some will actually try to do you harm. In this house, we have to be a real family. This house must be a refuge for us from the outside world. Never forget we are a family. We protect each other outside the house and love each other inside the house."

I have told my teams this same story. It works the same way with a team as it does with a family. "Outside our facility there are lots of people who want to see our team fail. Even some of your classmates who slap you on the back and say good job secretly are jealous and do not wish you the best."

"I work as a resource room teacher with children who have learning disabilities. A few years ago, a young boy began taking lessons in my resource room. I could not figure out what had brought him to seek my help. He clearly had no difficulty with his lessons and did well on all his tests. Yet, time after time he consistently came to my resource room for his lessons. I was determined to find his area of weakness but, as hard as I tried, I could

Culture Defeats Strategy 2 - Goonville, Texas Pop. 11

not find any type of learning disability or difficulty. Finally, out of frustration, I took him aside and told him I could not continue giving him lessons. It was a waste of his time and his parents' hard-earned money and he clearly did not need any sort of remedial help. The boy turned to me and said, "I will tell you why I am here, but I am asking you not to tell anyone else. I have a friend with a learning disability. Our teacher told him that he needed remedial classes in the resource room. He was so embarrassed to be singled out as having to go to your classes. I told him that it was no big deal and that I also take remedial classes. That is why I come to you, so that my friend will not be embarrassed."

This amazing example of empathy is from a 10-year old boy who just wanted to make his friend feel better about having a learning disability. He will be a leader one day because he will make sure others feel safe.

Empathy is much harder to teach than it is to model. Jeff Monken, Army head coach, did not get his team out for the national anthem before the Armed Forces Bowl in 2017. Think about it, a service academy team missed the national anthem for a bowl game!

Liz Roscher of Yahoo Sports describes how Coach Monken handled it. *When a football team isn't on the field when the national anthem plays, everybody wants to know why. But when that team is the Army Black Knights, everybody *really* wants to know why.*

We didn't have to wait long to find out what was going on. When Army coach Jeff Monken was interviewed at halftime, he explained what happened. And it's a lot more mundane than you might think. And this is what Monken said to the reporter:

Culture Defeats Strategy 2 - Goonville, Texas Pop. 11

"I want to apologize, I'm most embarrassed for not being out here for the national anthem. They had a five-minute push, we didn't realize it watching the clock. I want to apologize to all the soldiers, sailors and airmen out there. We had no intention of missing the national anthem. That's bothered me since we started the game."

Coach Monken showed true remorse for missing the anthem. He addressed it as quickly as possible to his players who signed up to defend and even die for the flag.

It is tough to hold your team accountable with an 'everything matters' mindset and have empathy for each situation. This is where the assistant coaches must have an open line of communication with their position players. When something truly comes up that needs to be taken into account, a coach with a real relationship will be able to have empathy.

3. The Head of the Family is an Encourager

While also in Minnesota for the MFCA clinic, I listened to Ian Shields, former head football coach at Jacksonville University, talk about the importance of and how all can be encouragers. "We think the term 'leader' can be intimidating to some, but all can be expected to encourage. Not all players can or want to take on the responsibility of being a team leader. On most teams, maybe 10% of the players have the mindset to do what it takes to be a captain or elite leader. Everyone, and I mean everyone can be a genuine encourager. We stress this and it is important to our culture."

Coach Shields is dead-on. Everyone doesn't want to be a leader on a team any more than everyone doesn't want

@CoachJacksonTPW #culturematters

to be a head coach, head principal, or manager of people in a business. When we say to our team, 'we need more leaders,' or 'everyone can lead in their own way,' it is subjective. If you tell them 'all of us must bring the juice and be vocal encouragers,' that doesn't sound like too much to ask.

The Encouragement Game

A few times a year we will place player names in a hat or helmet and have players draw them out. If we are in off-season every name will go in. If we are in-season we will have an offensive helmet and a defensive helmet. We tell them to make sure they don't draw out their name.

Next, they throw the paper away and do not tell anyone what name they picked. During practice, their job is to encourage the person they drew out of the hat. We tell them not to make it obvious, but to do a great job so at the end of practice, we ask each player in front of the group who they think drew out their name. This is an easy way to be intentional with encouragement. It also forces the introvert to get out of his comfort zone and open his mouth to lift up a teammate.

Mudita

Mudita is a Buddhist term or virtue that means 'finding joy in the happiness and success of others, usually rendered by unselfish, sympathetic, or altruistic joy.' While I am the farthest from a 'Buddhist anything,' I do believe in the power of words, and the concept of Mudita is powerful. Google "Mudita" and you will find a few 'Mudita award-winners' from various university teams.

Every team that has a few players who are genuinely happy when another player has success is fortunate. Culture drives behavior and our society does not celebrate Mudita, so we must do it.

Playing a team sport, it would seem obvious finding joy in others' success would be normal, but every coach reading this has seen 'that look' on faces of a few players who didn't play much after a big win. It is tough for me to handle and sometimes I can't contain myself without saying something.

So how do instill a culture of joy for others in our team? Like everything, it must be taught.

1. We teach them to take pride and pleasure in being a part of something bigger than themselves.

2. In practice (this will be discussed more in the next chapter), we encourage our guys to appreciate the ones who make them better. After practice, we ask them to recognize these guys.

3. The Houston Astros have a great routine after each win. Before showering they get together and recognize what each other did to accomplish the victory. "Jose did a great job converting the double play in the 7th inning to get us out of a jam." They go around the room allowing everyone to celebrate a teammate.

4. I'm positive I don't understand a lot about karma, but we will also stress to our guys the person who

complains about a bad pass thrown his way is usually the one who drops his next opportunity.

5. In our 2018 season, we started having a weekly Mudita Award Winner for each game. The more you celebrate something, the more you will get of it and every team needs more players who are joyful when a teammate succeeds. Maybe I will be able to find a large hand to represent a 'high-five' trophy they can keep in their locker for the week.

FIND A COMMUNITY MEMBER TO BE A SERVANT LEADER

Steven Carroll is our team chaplain and was our booster club president during the 2017 season at NF. He is 100% dedicated to serving our goons, and even though his son, Jordan, graduated in 2018, he has continued to be our chaplain and serve our booster club.

I wish everyone could have a booster club president with a heart like his. Steven had only one agenda, to help me and the rest of the staff get what we thought we needed to turn the program. His answer was always, "YES" when I asked for anything. He just wanted to serve everyone in the program and that's what he did.

Steven is an ordained minister so he has a heart to serve. Before I arrived, he also played music for the team at every practice. We use a drone to film practice, so I asked him to fly it for us, in true servant fashion he agreed and was there every morning.

He also serves the team away from school. He and his wife, Donna, have players over to their house for meals, allowed players to ride with them when they took Jordan to football camps in the summer, and will text players encouragement during the week.

Steven is a presence for us every day at practice and during every game. He is in our locker room leading the team prayer before the game, on our sideline during the game and either congratulating our guys or consoling them after the game.

Before coming to NF, I had another amazing team chaplain. John Earle served us unselfishly. He mentored, encouraged, and was another voice a kid could go to if they needed him. John was the first one who taught me how important it was to have this person for your team. Steven Carroll was already doing this when I arrived at NF, so I was lucky to inherit him.

Years ago, a head coach gave me the advice to 'keep my distance' from parents and the community as a whole as much as possible. "They will disappoint you most of the time. They all have an agenda, for their son and the next 10 best to play." Sadly, this is not the worst advice I have been given. Many parents do have 'strings-attached' motives that we must take into account when accepting anything from them. It takes a lot of discernment to decipher who to trust and from whom to keep your distance. If you are a coach and have a few years under your belt, there is probably one or two situations coming to mind right now of a parent who wanted something in return for their help.

So, I know this is easier said than done, but if you can find a non-coach community member to be another '1 of the 5,' do it. Allow them on your sideline and in your locker room. When you find the right person, he will add so much. He will be another servant that our kids and even young coaches need so badly.

A HEROIC WARRIOR WHO DID IT WHILE SERVING OTHERS

Desmond Doss was a conscientious objector when he was drafted to serve our military in WWII. When Pearl Harbor was attacked he was working at a naval shipyard in Virginia and could have opted to remain there, but he knew he wanted to serve, just without a gun.

"I am healthy. I need to serve and have the energy to do it as a medic," he said. In typical (some say) military fashion, Doss was assigned to a rifle company instead. Doss' refusal to shoot or even carry a weapon caused a lot of tension and strife with his company. They viewed him as a misfit and a coward. One even said to him, "Doss, as soon as we get into combat I am going to make sure you don't come back alive."

His commanding officers also had no use for him, believing a soldier without a gun was useless. They tried all they could to intimidate Doss by giving him extra duties, verbally abusing him, and even declaring him unfit to serve. Finally, they attempted to court martial him for refusing a direct order - to carry his weapon.

Doss wasn't being insubordinate in his eyes. He was raised with a strong belief in the bible and took the Ten Commandments literal. 'Thou shall not kill' was something he could not do.

They failed to get him kicked out and he refused to leave. Eventually, Doss was allowed to serve his fellow troops as a medic. Even those who had made his life difficult, he treated.

He served in the Pacific conflict, helping save lives on the islands of Guam, Leyte, and Okinawa. While others were taking lives, he was saving them. Whenever he heard, "medic!" on the battlefield, Doss consistently ran to the wounded soldier without regard for his own safety. He was so close to the enemy lines it was not unusual for him to hear the Japanese troops whispering to each other.

Doss' story was told in the 2016 movie 'Heartbreak Ridge.' This is another great movie clip you can use with your team when you are teaching on servant leadership. There are several great teachable clips from the film, but the most impactful one for me is when Doss disobeys orders to continue to go save others after retreating and the battlefield had been abandoned.

Culture Defeats Strategy 2 - Goonville, Texas Pop. 11

The battlefield was full of smoke and burning debris as the Japanese soldiers patrolled to look for American survivors to execute. Doss is still attempting to carry Americans to safety when he is going back to get his wounded sergeant. A bullet hits the top of his helmet and knocks him down. He gathers himself, puts the sergeant on his back and takes him to safety. As soon as he sets him down, he goes back to find another one. Each time he lowers them down a cliff tied to a rope to waiting soldiers who have no idea who is at the end of the rope at the top.

As he goes back to the battlefield, he hears a half-dead American mutter, "help me," "help me," as Japanese troops are mere feet away. Doss has to make a split-second decision and says, "trust me," to the wounded soldier and covers his face with dirt, only leaving his eye exposed. Doss then grabs a dead soldier and places on top of him to 'play dead' and give himself some cover as the Japanese walk right over their position.

An enemy soldier looks closely at the pile of bodies (where Doss is on the bottom), stops and bayonet's the dead body on top of Doss, barely missing him. Eventually, the Japanese move on, he grabs the wounded American and lowers him to safety.

In a documentary on his life, Doss says, "I was praying the whole time. I just kept praying, 'Lord, please help me get one more.'"

After Doss' heroic feat in Okinawa, his commander told him that he rescued 100 men. Doss said that the number could only be 50 at most. So, the official compromise was 75.

The Medal of Honor was established during the Civil War under President Abraham Lincoln in 1862. At the 100-year anniversary of the MOH celebration in 1962, the other recipients selected Desmond Doss to represent them at a White House ceremony. Not only was he the only conscientious objector to ever win our nation's highest honor, but he was selected by the other winners (there have been only 462 medals ever awarded) to represent them at the White House. Doss was a true servant leader hero. Tell his story to your team. They need to hear it.

CHAPTER 5 REVIEW
LEADERS EAT LAST

- Seniority is a responsibility, not a privilege. A great culture must include a 'leaders eat last' mindset throughout.

- Find ways to celebrate the 'water-carriers' on your team. Challenge them to carry in an underclassmen's pads once a week for example.

- What is celebrated will be repeated.

- The easiest part of coaching is putting on the whistle. One of the most important parts is serving the players we have.

- Carry Your Shield to protect your teammate(s).

- Leaders have empathy for those under them.

- Mudita is special but will only happen if you celebrate it.

- Find a community member to help your staff pour into players.

CHAPTER 6
LESSON #5 – PRACTICE IS EVERYTHING

> *"I love practice. It is when a coach exercises the most control over the improvement of his or her team."*
>
> Mike Krzyzewski
> Men's Basketball Coach
> Duke University

John Earle, our chaplain at Grapevine, told me this story about experience in the NFL. "Everything is tough for undrafted free agents in the league. Guys like me have to find some kind of way to make an impression and 'bring it' every day. We had to take care of ourselves because as soon as you were injured you were going to be cut. Each morning I was one of the first in the training room to get taped and treated for any minor injury. Guys like me (rookie free agents) had to wait to get our ankles taped if there were veterans in the training room. If you were an early bird you could get taped and whatever else you needed done and not worry about it."

"One day, early in camp, after leaving the training room I walked to the locker room to get dressed and ready for practice. It was completely dark so I figured I was the first one in there. I found my way to my locker and put my things down." John continued, "when I turned around Tim Krumrie was sitting at the locker right across from mine in full pads and chewing on his mouthpiece. He was just staring right at me and not saying a word. Tim was an eight-year veteran at the time who had been All-Pro multiple times. He was waiting for me to arrive so he could intimidate me before practice that day. I thought, C'mon man! Give me a break, I am trying to just make the team!"

"That day I knew Tim was going to give me all he had and of course, he did. Here is the difference in an All-Pro's mindset versus a high school player's mindset: Tim wanted my best so I could get him better. He wasn't trying to get me to quit or make me have nightmares, he was playing mind games to get me to go harder against him. He scared me, he always went 100 miles per hour," John told me.

John was drafted in the 11th round from Western Illinois by the Cincinnati Bengals. He played in both the NFL and Canadian Football League for five years. I have had him tell this story to my teams at Grapevine and North Forney. The great ones don't just get through practice ... they attack it.

You are reading this book to get an edge. I have tried to make both books as 'bright lines' as possible. I dislike reading anything that doesn't give specific tools and techniques to improve either myself or my team. Core values will give your team an edge. The daily 'fist-fight' with classroom meetings to sell your core values will give your team an edge. Real relationship-building will give your team an edge. Attention to detail and an 'everything matters' mindset will give your team an edge. But, your team must prepare differently than your opponents to get this edge.

PRACTICE VS. TRAINING

Practice is defined as – 'performing an activity or exercise (a skill) repeatedly or regularly in order to improve or maintain one's proficiency. A form of learning through repetition.

Sometimes I hear the word training instead of practice and have wondered 'what's the difference between the two?' "You don't rise to the occasion, you fall to the level of your training," is a commonly used quote credited to the Navy Seals.

Training is defined as the acquisition of knowledge, skills, and competencies as a result of the teaching of vocational or practical skills and knowledge.

Words have impact and I have always thought 'training' was a pretty cool word. Training seems more military or official than the word practice. I may be 'picking nits' by comparing the two terms, but it's important we know there's a difference so we can make sure our teams are getting the most out of both.

Training is when you learn the skill and practice is when you go perform what you know for improvement. How does this apply to coaching? We shouldn't be teaching skills on the practice field. That is wasting precious time and reps. Coaches should teach and train their players before they go to the field so there is no wasted time during a practice session.

> **"Practice puts brains in your muscles."**
> **Sam Snead**
> **Professional Golfer**

ONLY DELIBERATE PRACTICE MAKES US BETTER

"The little things," "attention to detail" and "everything matters" are phrases I use a lot. They're all important because they're reminders of practicing deliberately.

Anders Ericsson is an 'expert on experts.' Originally from Sweden, he's now a professor of psychology at Florida State University, and has studied expert spellers, athletes, musicians, and other elite performers. In his findings, Ericsson determined the key to achieving mastery is intentional or deliberate practice.

Ericsson, with fellow researchers, first published work on deliberate practice in 1993. They studied 40 German violinists to attempt to determine if they could find factors that differentiated the elite from the good or mediocre. The violinists gave the researchers detailed records of how they spent their time, not only on music practice, but other activities as well. Ericsson and his colleagues found that the elite violinists spent significantly more hours practicing alone than the good or mediocre ones. Next, they did the same study with pianists and found the same results.

The problem with the study is that it did not specify what type of practice the musicians were engaged in.

Culture Defeats Strategy 2 - Goonville, Texas Pop. 11

You have to dig deeper, which Ericsson did, to understand the practice has to be deliberate.

Deliberate practice can be described as having a specific goal of something you want to improve. It is purposeful, systematic, and follows a pattern. Author James Clear says that deliberate practice is when you "break down the process into parts, identify your weaknesses, test new strategies for each section, and integrate your learning into the overall process." Clear says that Ben Hogan is known in some golf circles as 'inventing practice' because he broke down the swing in parts and figured out how to master each with methodical practice.

Hogan loved to practice. He's historically one of the greatest golfers of all time with nine major victories. In Clear's blog on deliberate practice he quotes Hogan, *"I couldn't wait to get up in the morning so I could hit balls. I'd be at the practice tee at the crack of dawn, hit balls for a few hours, then take a break and get right back to it."*

Clear goes on to say, "*For Hogan, every practice session had a purpose. He reportedly spent years breaking down each phase of the golf swing and testing new methods for each segment. The result was near perfection. He developed one of the most finely-tuned golf swings in the history of the game.*"

Using Ericsson's research as his foundation, author Malcolm Gladwell, determined the 'gold standard' for becoming an expert at a skill is 10,000 hours. In his book "Outliers," published in 2008, Gladwell argues that the key to become world-class is a matter of practicing for a total of 10,000 hours.

Culture Defeats Strategy 2 - Goonville, Texas Pop. 11

Let's use basketball as an example of what these researchers are saying. Deliberate practice would be a shooter who shoots 300 shots, with a buddy to help him retrieve the ball. He not only keeps a record of shots made and missed, but also how the shot was missed i.e., if the shot was short, long, left or right, etc. After each session, the shooter reviews the data and then repeats the process. On the other end of the court, another player shoots 100 shots without anyone to help him. He leisurely dribbles between shots, walks to get missed shots and takes frequent breaks.

One of the biggest challenges we have as coaches is making sure the drills we use are 'game-like'. A great drill is one a coach can reference when watching game film with his players. At NF, we are a rugby tackling team. I believe the rugby tackling technique will help save the game of football by taking the head out of tackling. The normal, 'old school' way to teach tackling is 'head across the bow' (or head in front of the ball carrier), but in rugby tackling defenders track to hip and place the head behind the hip. Rugby players do not wear helmets so the only way they could tackle is without their head.

One of our best ways to practice rugby tackling deliberately is with a tackling circuit. In the circuit, our guys work different types of techniques which are determined by the position they are in relation to the ball carrier. One of the fundamentals in each tackling technique is to 'run and gather,' stay square and track the near hip.

Culture Defeats Strategy 2 - Goonville, Texas Pop. 11

> *"Most people get excited about games, but I've got to be excited about practice, because that's my classroom."*
>
> **Pat Summit**
> **Women's Basketball Coach**
> **University of Tennessee**

Ryan Porter, our defensive coordinator, explains how deliberate we teach certain aspects of tackling, "it's just like a 'tight-turn' tackling drill where you use near-foot strike technique. You have to get your feet under you and be under control." We should all ask ourselves if we have drills that we never comment on when going over game film with our team. If the drill isn't seen in a game then it is not deliberate practice.

Ericsson says Gladwell has missed the boat or misinterpreted the 10,000 rule because he does not factor in the importance of deliberate practice. Without a system of intentional improvement, we are just spending more time on the activity.

Without a system, we are just practicing 'naively.' Naïve practice is where we just go play. There is no instruction, only time spent. We're only gaining more experience. We're like the golfer who just wants to play a round of golf each Saturday and never practice his short game or work on the range. With deliberate practice, he could get 100 putts in a short time whereas he will only putt 30+ times in a four-hour round.

Mindless activity is the enemy of deliberate practice. Just because we are practicing something over and over only means we are enforcing a habit. One of my personality flaws is lack of patience (everyone reading this book who knows me is yelling 'amen' in their brain

Culture Defeats Strategy 2 - Goonville, Texas Pop. 11

right now) so when I see something wrong on the practice field I cannot help myself. I have heard head coaches talk about making a note of 'these wrongs' and discussing them in the post-practice staff meeting. For me, it's just reinforcing a bad habit and needs to be fixed right when it happens. This is a rare thing with our coaching staff because we meet before we go out and are always on the same page but with so many moving parts it does happen on occasion.

A fascinating story of 'practicing wrong' is one I heard on a podcast a couple of years ago about a couple of police officers practicing disarming a gunman.

> **"Repetition alone is inaccurate. It is not a matter of repeating, but the nature of what is being repeated."**
>
> **James Smith**

Two officers were training on how to disarm a gunman. One officer stuck a fake pistol out and the other officer quickly hit him across the forearm, turned his wrist and took the weapon from him. Then, to get as many reps as they could, he handed the pistol right back to him so they could immediately go again. Over the course of time each officer went through this scenario thousands of times getting several reps per minute.

One day, when they were actually on patrol, an actual situation occurred where a real gunman stuck out a real gun. Training took over and the officer hit him across the forearm, turned his wrist and took the pistol from him. Just as quickly, he *handed it back to the gunman!*

All the reps were great for disarming the assailant but he also practiced giving the weapon back thousands of times and that is exactly what he did when it was 'game time.'

PRACTICE PREPARATION

> *"The absolute bottom line in coaching is organization and preparing for practice."*
>
> **Bill Walsh**
> **Head Coach**
> **San Francisco 49ers**

One of the main goals of pre-practice planning by any staff is to prevent mindless practice, slow practice and incorrect practice.

Practice needs to be a performance or a 'symphony'. We get a few high school coaches and college recruiters who come visit us at NF. I am always very proud when they say they're impressed by our practice tempo and structure.

This can only happen if we're organized by meeting as a staff daily. Our meetings are a fairly formal affair so we are efficient and focused. We have a set of four tables pushed together to form one large table for all of us to sit around. To help create the 'business-like' atmosphere all coaches have an assigned seat and I ask them to keep their cell phones in their pockets. We don't do this so I can feel like 'Mr. Big,' we do it to have the correct mindset while we're meeting. We will laugh, cut-up and have light-hearted moments, but for the most part it's time to plan either a practice or off-season workout. Both are serious business that determine the program's future.

Culture Defeats Strategy 2 - Goonville, Texas Pop. 11

"You mean to tell me your staff meets every morning at 6:30 ... in January?" Dr. Rob Gilbert, creator of the Success Hotline, called me one morning while we were meeting to prepare for phase 1 of offseason in the second semester. Because we begin track workouts at 7:00 am we must meet at 6:00 or 6:15. Dr. Gilbert is a professor of sports psychology at Montclair State University in New Jersey. We are lucky in Texas to get an 'athletic period' each day so we get to have intense workouts in-season and out-of-season. Every workout must be planned beforehand so we can attack each minute.

This is not the most fun part of coaching, but for practice to look like a 'well-oiled machine' staffs must meet and plan every minute of it. Pete Carroll talks about this on his video 'Practice is Everything.' "Organization starts with the coaches. We must always meet first with an attention to detail mindset so there is no wasted time."

When our players leave each afternoon, our staff will sit down and plan practice for the next day. We do not have a lot of variance from week to week but we do have differences in our daily schedule.

CORRECT REPETITION MAKES THE DIFFERENCE

In 1934, after nine military pilots died in a 20-day span, President Roosevelt had had enough and asked the U.S. Air Corp commander, "when are these killings going to stop?"

The U.S. was still in the infancy of pilot training. Its foundational belief was that good pilots are 'born, not made.' Most programs began with taking a recruit up in a plane and the instructor executing a series of loops and rolls. If the student didn't get sick, he was on his way. They believed he had what it took to be a military pilot.

High fatality rates had always been the norm in U.S. military training schools. In 1912, eight of 14 pilots died in crashes. Training had gotten a little better by '34 but not much. FDR believed there had to be a better way to learn to fly. There was, and it was from what was perceived as a child's toy at the time.

Edward Link paid $50 for a flying lesson in 1920 when he was 16 years old. "For the better part of that hour we did the Sweet Spot 21 loops and spins and buzzed everything in sight," Link recalled later. "Thank heaven I didn't get sick, but when we got down, I hadn't touched the controls at all. I thought, 'That's a hell of a way to teach someone to fly'."

Link wasn't deterred and eventually purchased a four-seat Cessna, but he still kept thinking there had to be a way to improve pilot training. He grew working in his dad's piano factory so he borrowed pneumatic pumps and bellows and built what was later called a "blue box." It looked somewhat like a plane with its small wings and tail. The box had an instrument panel and electric motor that would allow it to roll, pitch and yaw like a regular plane. When the pilot made an error, a small light on the nose would light up.

Link named it the 'Link Aviation Trainer' and advertised that using it he could teach students to fly in half the time and a fraction of the cost of traditional training. It was a brilliant invention that would revolutionize how pilots learned to fly.

The problem was in 1927 no one thought it was a good idea and it was rejected by everyone. Link couldn't get anyone to purchase a trainer; not the military academies or private flying schools. The U.S. Patent Office deemed it "a novel, profitable amusement device." In the early 1930s, Link was hauling one of his trainers on a flatbed truck to county fairs and charging 25 cents a ride.

When Link was contacted by the military to give a demonstration of his trainer he flew and landed perfectly in foggy, stormy weather that had grounded all other flyers. Desperate times call for desperate measures so although they still weren't sure if this arcade game would help train real pilots, the military purchased their first shipment of Link trainers.

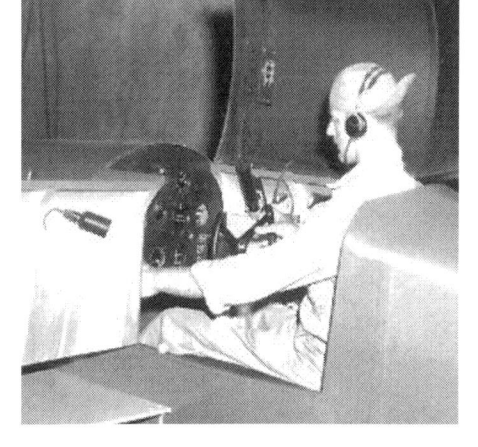

The 'blue box' worked perfectly. It allowed pilots to practice more deliberately and deeply. They were able to make errors, learn from them, and then go again. In just a few hours, a pilot could take off, land, dive, stall, and recover over and over again. By the end of World War II, 500,000 pilots had trained on 10,000 Link trainers.

I read this story from one of my all-time favorite books, 'The Talent Code' by Daniel Coyle. As he explains, the pilots using the trainer were no smarter, or better than the ones dying prior to using it. They were simply getting more repetitions. It would be like thinking you are going to become a great putter but you only putt when you are playing a round of golf. It doesn't work that way.

Practice Rep to Game Rep Ratio

Mike Neighbors, head women's basketball coach at the University of Arkansas, believes the correct 'practice to play' ratio is 5 to 1. "It's very hard to get the number of practice reps needed for skill development if a player is playing 100 summer league games," said Coach Neighbors.

This ratio is right on the money. If you are going to run any offensive play in a game the minimum number of reps practiced during the week should be five. Inside zone is one of our 'hat rack' plays. It varies from week to week but on average we will call it 10+ times per game. If we ran it 12 times against any opponent then the ratio means we should have practiced it 60 times throughout the week.

Overlearn - 'Monotony brings home the bacon'

Don Shula, the Hall of Fame coach of the Miami Dolphins for 26 years, wrote years ago; *"we must practice something so much we 'overlearn' it. He said, "constant practice, constant attention to detail every time produces hunger to be in the middle of the action. When players have absolutely **no doubt** about what*

Culture Defeats Strategy 2 - Goonville, Texas Pop. 11

they're supposed to do or how to do it, they thrive on pressure.

You play at the level you practice. The best way to excel is to practice hard all the time. I'm convinced that both the coaches and the players must know that the overlearning system works. That means they must understand all four of the components:

a. Limit the number of goals

b. Make people master their assignments

c. Reduce players' practice errors

d. Strive for continuous improvement

A team is ready for peak play because their energy is not drained away by worry about mechanical trifles – 'what-do-I-do-whens.' When these interferences are eliminated players are more likely to get into a "zone" where peak performance is possible."

I read Coach Shula's concept of overlearning over 20 years ago (if only I had continued to read like I do now). He co-authored with Ken Blanchard a business leadership book titled, 'Everyone's A Coach.' Immediately after reading about the 'overlearn' philosophy I thought it applied directly to defensive players running to the ball. Back when teams were huddling up between plays defensive coaches had a little time to teach pursuit. We had all 11 members of our defense 'swarm' the ball, defensive coaches would 'throw' them towards the ball if we had to. Our thought was if they did it every play in practice then they wouldn't have to think about it in a game. When we

Culture Defeats Strategy 2 - Goonville, Texas Pop. 11

think, we play slower. Every now and then we would even see one of our players 'buzz his feet' at the pile when reviewing game film on Saturday morning (just like they did at practice).

It has been said that when one is given no time to think, they will react as they have been trained. This is true 100000%! We all fall to the level of our training when the bullets are flying.

THE SCIENCE BEHIND MUSCLE MEMORY - MYELIN

> *"It's time to rewrite the maxim that practice makes perfect. The truth is, practice makes myelin, and myelin makes perfect."*
> — Daniel Coyle

Daniel Coyle explains simply in 'The Talent Code' how our body reacts to repeated, intentional practice. Skill development movements, like those that occur when a pilot is training in a simulator, works so well because all the repetitions change our neural circuits. After hours of deliberate practice, we develop muscle memory. Overlearning is another term for muscle memory. It's the ability to reproduce a particular movement without conscious thought, acquired as a result of frequent repetition of that movement.

Muscle memory is possible because of a white substance called myelin. Myelin is insulation that grows around neural circuits. Every time our brain sends a command to 'fire' a circuit the more myelin grows around it. An increase in myelin is an increase in the speed and accuracy of our muscle fibers. Myelin helps our muscles know what to do, allowing us to execute more complicated skills, but it only works if we keep affecting our nerve circuits through deliberate repetitions.

When you do something that is 'so easy it's like riding a bike' you have created muscle memory which is actually strands of myelin.

THE SCIENCE BEHIND LEARNING - SPACED REPETITION

You learn a lot when you get your first head coaching job. There is just no way to prepare for all the 'stuff' that comes with running a football program. I was given my first chance to be in charge in Paducah, Texas circa 1999. Paducah is a wonderful, but arid community in West Texas.

> *"They tell you no one is perfect. Then they tell you practice makes perfect. I wish they'd make up their mind."*
>
> **Winston Churchill**

'Other duties assigned' is at the bottom of coaching contracts. It pretty much means whatever needs to be done. We all know it comes with the territory. It comes back to 'putting on the whistle' is the easiest part of coaching.

Watering the game field in Paducah was something I needed to make sure happened. Healthy turf is a serious requirement and not to be taken lightly. I learned if you water every day the grass will look healthy, but the root system will not go deep. A deep watering of 1" (an empty tuna can) once a week will force the roots to drive down during the latter part of the week to search for moisture. The grass isn't quite as green but the root system is much stronger.

The same is true for how we learn. The brain also needs the correct interval or spacing for maximum learning. Most people think our brains operate similar to a computer. A computer stores whatever information we command it to store, but we cannot command our brain to remember.

The brain cannot effectively store and recall a lot of information in a short period of time. This is why 'cramming' for a test is the worst method of learning. The brain keeps what it deems to be important. The more the brain encounters memories or thoughts on a regular basis the more it will remember them. So, in reality, unless we 'hack' the brain we do not have direct control over how much we remember.

To get our brain to remember the most effectively we must space out when we give it information. The spacing should be at set intervals over time. We should teach our guys a new scheme or play and then come back to it on a regular basis. When we do this, we are 'hacking' the brain's learning capacity.

I was able to visit the Dallas Cowboys practice facility a couple of years ago during the season. The schedule they had for that day was:

Culture Defeats Strategy 2 - Goonville, Texas Pop. 11

6:30-8:00 am	Weight room open and breakfast
7:00 am	Training room open
7:30-8:25 am	Special teams meetings /B'fast club
8:30-8:40 am	Special teams walk thru
8:45-10:30 am	O/D meetings-walk thru
11:00-1:00 pm	Practice
1:15-2:45 pm	Lunch / Weight room / media
2:45-4:15 pm	Offense/Defense meetings

None of us have the time of a professional football team, but it is worth noting how much spaced repetition there is in the Cowboys' schedule: meetings, walk thru, practice, meetings.

The other days of the week we only practice once but we bring them back after school to lift weights and review video of the morning session. Physically they are not getting reps of inside zone footwork, but mentally they are. This is also important. Twice a day Monday and Tuesday our players are learning their assignments in the morning and after school.

WALK-THRU

We are a 'one word call' team. To help us play as fast as possible (many teams use this system) we can say one word and it will tell our guys the formation, play and play direction (left or right). Not only is it important to have two sessions some days with our players, but we also space out reps during a practice. Spacing out our one-word calls at different times during our training session hacks the brain as well.

@CoachJacksonTPW #culturematters

We begin every practice with a 7 – 8-minute walk through. The physical intensity is low but we demand mental focus. We are locking them in mentally by going over as many of our plays we have on our practice script as we can. They are jogging which also warms their muscles up as they are going through each play in their head.

If we are doing something for the first time, like our first spring practice in 2017, we will do a coach's walk-through and a total team walk through.

TRAINING IS FOR TEACHING – PRACTICE IS FOR DOING

Chip Kelly, head football coach at UCLA, has been known as an innovator for years. Kelly's teams always play with great tempo which means they must practice with tempo. Jayson Hron wrote an article for USA Hockey titled, *'Go Fast and Take Chances: Football Innovator's Techniques Work Well on the Ice.'*

"I don't care what it is, but when they get to practice, they better be doing something," Kelly said. "When players get to the practice field, it's practice time. That period is not a walk-thru period we can teach in a classroom. The practice field is not where we talk. It's where we do skills. We want to keep the words to a minimum. The words you do use must have meaning. Players don't want to hear you give a 10-minute clinic in the middle of the field."

Years ago, I heard Gary DiNardo, when he was the head football coach at LSU, say that it is bad coaching for a coach to write things on the board during his meeting

Culture Defeats Strategy 2 - Goonville, Texas Pop. 11

time with his unit or anything he couldn't have written before his players arrived. I remember thinking, 'wow, this guy doesn't waste any time.' This is how we must look at training and practice. Meetings, film review and walk-thru sessions are when we are training. When practice starts it needs to be a 'hair on fire' event.

"We emphasize what it is and we coach it," said Kelly. "It really bothers me when I go to a high school practice and something is being done without any intention. The entire team is stretching, and the coaches are standing around talking to one another or throwing the ball around. If stretching is important they should show with their actions it is important. If you don't think stretching is important, don't do it. If you do think it's important, you have to show your team it's important."

We don't have any drills in practice that aren't important. There are two speeds for us; learning and game. When we hit the field, we are going to be in game speed most of the time.

In our team warm up, our offensive skill players have a ball and we have coaches wearing boxing gloves and 'crayon' arm pads trying to knock the ball loose. We even have a couple of sticks with boxing gloves taped to the end of them trying to create fumbles. For any ball that hits the ground the entire team does an up-down.

When practice starts it is serious business. When researching this chapter I found an article where a coach says, 'Start practice by having the kids running laps to warm up. This allows the coaches to get organized, and set up the field to get practice started.'

Culture Defeats Strategy 2 - Goonville, Texas Pop. 11

For the love of God, your players deserve better than that and if you want practice to be meaningful, it must be from the 'get go'.

"When practice starts until practice ends, we practice as hard as we can," said Coach Kelly. "We practice fast and we finish everything."

> *"When you prepare for everything, you're ready for anything."*
> **Bill Walsh**
> **Head Football Coach**
> **San Francisco 49ers**

IF IT HAPPENS IN THE GAME, IT MUST BE PRACTICED

Work on situations in practice as much as possible. The 'money' down in football is 3rd down. We call it the 'cash' down and have our guys make the Johnny Manziel cash sign with their hands and yell, "cash, cash, cash!" We have to practice this to make it happen or it won't happen in the game. Our booster club bought large '$' signs and they participate with us during games.

Bill Parcells writes in his book, 'Finding a Way to Win' when he was trying to break into NFL coaching he was hired to analyze why the Jets were near the bottom of the league in red zone offensive production. After looking at how they practice, he told them they don't work goal line situations near enough. After they committed to more red zone time during the week, the following season they were near the top in goal line offense.

Culture Defeats Strategy 2 - Goonville, Texas Pop. 11

Coach Bill Walsh says in his book, 'The Score Takes Care of Itself', *"Making judgments under severe stress is the most difficult thing there is. The more preparation you have prior to the conflict, the more you can do in a clinical situation, the better off you will be. For that reason, in practice I want to make certain that we have accounted for every critical situation, including the desperate ones at the end of a game when we may have only one chance to pull out a victory. Even in that circumstance, I want us to have a play prepared and rehearsed. Say it is the last 20 seconds of a game and we're losing. We have already practiced six plays that we can apply in that situation. That way, we know what to do, and we can calmly execute the plays. We'll have no doubt in our minds, we will have more poise, and we can concentrate without falling prey to desperation."*

"You need to have a plan even for the worst scenario. It doesn't mean that it will always work; it doesn't mean that you will always be successful. But you will always be prepared and at your best."

Chad Morris has a 4/4 principle that states teams that win the last four minutes of the first half and the first four minutes of the second half win 88% of their games. Mark Smith, former cornerback coach for the Hogs told me, "The three years we were at SMU and the two years at UA 4/4 held up. Every game we won we also won 4/4." This is an amazing statistic and only reinforces what we've all heard and preached to our teams for years, "the first drives for the offense and defense of the second half are the most important of the game."

If it is so important then we should practice it. We have a 7-minute halftime during each of our practices. We compete right before the halftime with 1 v. 1 drills and then our players will get with their 'family groups,' sit around the field wherever the coach in charge of the group wants to be, and talk about our leadership topic of the week.

When halftime is over we do a one minute warm-up, a condensed version of what happens in a game. Coach Luster, who warms them up before we run through the tunnel on game night, warms them up at practice and makes it as similar as possible.

After this brief warm-up, we will do one repetition of either kickoff or kickoff return then go 'good on good, 11 v. 11 team session, just like what happens on game night. It's powerful for me to say to our team, "we know the first four minutes of the second half are so important. We practice it every day so let's go do our thing."

If it happens in a game then it is important. This may be considered a small thing by some, but time outs happen so we must practice them. During fall camp, we work on how we will conduct timeouts, how our 'O' and 'D' will gather on the sideline after a change of possession. We will even practice how we will align for the national anthem (numerical order). Great basketball coaches will work on their full and 30-second timeout routine well before the first game.

This past season I wasn't pleased with our half-time system so I did what I always do: I reached out to a few coaches and asked how they do half-time. Our routine became much more structured after this. We changed in the middle of the season so we practiced half-time the week of the change. We didn't just talk about it and hope we would execute the changes.

TEMPO - PRACTICE UNDER PRESSURE

"We play with maniacal effort that makes their butts quit." This is part of our credo and how we define 'Falcon Fast.' When I arrived, they didn't move fast. It was part of our daily fist-fight (and always will be) to get them to have a sense of urgency in everything they do. After I had been there for a few weeks I decided to have a competition to see who could put their shoes on the quickest.

This is an effective activity to do with your team to stress the importance of moving fast. As they sat in their rows I had them take off their shoes and untie them. I blew a whistle and timed them to see how quick (or slow) we were at getting our shoes back on and tied. The results were varied of course, but it was an eye-opener for them to not only see who did not move fast but reinforced our 'everything matters' mantra. You could even have this as a competition at the end of workout to see who gets to go to the showers first.

This past spring (2019) during our boot camp I also timed them on getting dressed and standing at attention in front of their locker. In boot camp, we are going to take control from the 'get go'. We had each grade go at separate times so no one would 'fall through the cracks' and we miss them. For example, the rising seniors would be in the hall waiting on the whistle. When the whistle blew they had *70 seconds* to get dressed and stand in front of their clean locker at attention. Anyone who did not make the time had to go to another locker down the hall for that day. It was intense and we were moving Falcon Fast!

Our practices are as up-tempo and pressure-packed as we can make them. If you want to sleep well the night before your game you must make practice a daily 'event.' The games take care of themselves when the week of prep is organized, extremely fast-paced and there is constant pressure applied to your players to perform.

We Must Coach Fast to Practice Fast

Just like the Link Trainer, we have to find ways for our players to get as many reps as possible in varied situations. One way to do this is to make sure we are not slowing practice down by stopping the action and talking too much. The Link Trainer does not force the pilot to sit there and listen to a recording for minutes at a time. The pilot gets feedback with a flashing light on the nose of the plane when a correction should be made. Coaches should similarly give feedback, short and to the point, so another rep can take place.

John Wooden used the 'sandwich technique' of correction. It was very quick also. When a mistake in practice was made he would say what should have happened, not the mistake he did see and again what should have happened. 'Do this, not that, do this.' For example, "near foot strike, not off balance, near foot strike." This is quick and emphasizes what is correct technique.

We still must give feedback after every rep.

This is a BIG pet-peeve of mine. Do not ask your athlete to give you everything he or she has with total effort and not give them constant feedback. You may be thinking, 'you just said don't talk too much and now you are saying talk to them after every rep?' Give them short bursts of feedback and let them go again.

We love coaching or we wouldn't be doing it. But too much verbiage can slow down the pace of practice. We can give them constant feedback between reps without hindering the tempo. For us, offensively, we are going to run a play every 15-20 seconds in a team situation. This means coaches have about eight seconds to give feedback as our guys are lining up.

Coach fast, film practice, and go over it with your team afterwards in a meeting situation. The time for coaches to 'hear themselves talk' (but always asking questions like Coach Callahan of Minnesota) is during video review and not on the field. We should use short phrases like, "sink your hips," or "come to balance." These are tackling corrections in which players totally understand the message. There is no need to say, "Make sure you don't overrun the ball carrier here. You need to use our near foot strike technique in this situation." This takes too long. Give them feedback and let them go again!

Games are pressure environments — It can't be when they feel it first

Back to the '17 game at Poteet. There was not a last-second play that decided it, but there were several big plays that turned the tide for us. Two of them were 4th down plays (we went for it 47 times on 4th down in 2017) where QB Colby Suits completed passes to Cory Mayfield. Corey is currently a starting defensive back at the University of Texas-San Antonio. Corey was one of our two-way players. Like any game, there were lots of big plays made throughout, but if we don't convert both 4th and long plays, we probably don't win. There was pressure for everyone, including the coaches. Coach Bachtel and Coach Wallis didn't overthink things. They commiserated and called base plays they were comfortable with, and our players executed them.

This is just one example of several throughout a wonderful season of guys coming through in the clutch for us. Game day is always going to be stressful. The more we can make practice stressful and add pressure to our athletes, the more they will be used to it.

How do you prepare your players to play under pressure?

1. Feeling of Control

In the article 'The Secret to Handling Pressure like Astronauts, Navy SEALs, and Samurai' by Eric Barker, it maps out how these organizations handle high-stress situations. *The first thing they look for is finding people who won't panic 150 miles above the earth.' Anything that gives them a feeling of control helps with performance and lessens feeling of panic.*

Walk-through's are great ways to give a feeling of control to your players. If we are doing something new, like before our first-ever spring practice in 2017, our coaches did a walk-thru on the practice field and went through every station. The next day our coaches and players went through it again. When it was time to go the following day, we practiced much faster and everyone was much more comfortable because we had walked through it.

Our pre-practice walk-thru sessions also help accomplish this. They get to ask questions and feel success before we are in our normal practice pace and moving '100 mph.'

2. Apply Pressure as Needed

"No big deal, Rusty. There's nothing riding on this snap...except maybe your damn scholarship." I was a sophomore at Northeast Louisiana University (now ULM) when head coach Pat Collins made this statement to a good friend of mine, Rusty Haile, as we were practicing field goals one day. Rusty was a great snapper that never had any issues so Coach Collins was just 'throwing it out there' to put some pressure on him. I remember thinking, 'oh crap, I'm rooting for you, Rusty.'

Good coaches find ways to see who can handle pressure. They put them in the situations as many times as they can before it counts on the scoreboard.

While I was visiting the Minnesota spring practice mentioned earlier I watched Coach Fleck squirt water to distract his kicker and holder during field goal attempts. He also tried to get a punt returner discombobulated by throwing a blocking dummy at them as they fielded the ball. Such tactics are designed for players to be quick and decisive when the plays start counting for real. "We put them in situations that you'd like to say will be harder here than in a game", he told the coaches.

Coach Steve Devoursney, head coach of the Cairo Syrupmakers in Cairo, Georgia, told me they squirt water on punt and kickoff returners during practice to make them focus on catching balls under stress.

Another great tactic I saw from the Gophers was how they added pressure to punt returners during a drill. Each time a returner came up he had one ball under each arm pit as a ball was shot out of a Jugs machine. If he caught the ball great but if he didn't he had to immediately drop both balls he was holding and 'grenade dive' on the ball he dropped. It is not fun to leave your feet and dive on a ball. It takes effort and is a little painful landing on the turf.

Our baseball coach, Tommy Sparks, has our team play '21 Outs.' He puts them through every situation a game could present. The team must execute 21 straight outs without making a mental or physical error or they start over.

"The pressure builds after we get to 15 or 16. No one wants to be that guy who boots a ball or throws to the wrong base and makes us start over," Coach Sparks told me.

Author, Ryan Holiday, writes about pressure practice in an article, '21 Life Lessons Learned from the World's Greatest Sports Coaches'. My favorite example is from Phil Jackson. He describes one of his most effective tactics when he prepares his players: "Once I had the Bulls practice in silence; on another occasion, I made them scrimmage with the lights out. Not because I want to make their lives miserable but because I want to prepare them for the inevitable chaos that occurs the minute they step onto a basketball court." Chaos, both in sports and in life, is inevitable. Are you prepared? How can you practice in advance so it doesn't catch you off guard?"

3. Teach Them How to Stay Calm with Controlled Breathing and to Park It

Brian Cain is my 'all things mental game' mentor. I mention him several times in CDS 1 and will always be grateful for him pulling back the curtain on how to get the edge in today's athletic world. Brian is an expert on helping athletes and coaches achieve peak mental performance.

One world-class aspect of Brian's training is how to teach your athletes (and yourself) to stay calm in pressure situations. Like everything, if it's going to happen in a game, we must practice it! We need everyone to stay calm under pressure so our job is to give them ways to do it.

Controlled Breathing - The #1 method to slow your mind and heart rate is to intentionally slow your breathing.

We do 6 - 2 - 8 controlled breathing routines at two different situations during a game. During timeouts and when either our offense or defense comes over to the sideline.

a. To execute a 6 - 2 - 8, inhale through your nose, deeply, expanding your stomach for a count of six - one, two, three, four, five, six.

b. Hold that breath in for a count of two - one, two.

c. Slowly exhale through your mouth, completely, contracting your stomach for a count of eight - one, two, three, four, five, six, seven, eight.

Culture Defeats Strategy 2 - Goonville, Texas Pop. 11

Through controlled breathing, you get more air into your lungs and more oxygen out to your body and brain. High levels of oxygen in your blood stream lower the body's demand for blood, which lowers heart rate. The breaths have to be deep, abdominal breaths where you expand your stomach like a balloon, pause at the top of the breath, then exhale while counting.

Sometimes it's tough for me to wait on the breathing before I speak to them, but I know it's beneficial to them to decrease their heart rate.

Try this exercise yourself to see the affect it will have on you. Simply take your heart rate shortly before employing this method, and then measure your heart rate again shortly after completing the 6 - 2 - 8 breathing exercise. This is definitely one of the more unconventional things we do, but if you'll try it with your team, they'll love it.

> *"Your breathing should flow gracefully, like a river, like a water snake crossing the water, and not like a chain of rugged mountains or the gallop of a horse. To master our breath is to be in control of our bodies and minds. Each time we find ourselves dispersed and find it difficult to gain control of ourselves by different means, the method of watching the breath should always be used."*
>
> **Thich Nhat Hanh**
> **Author, The Miracle of Mindfulness**

Park It - We use 'park it' as a way to teach our guys to let go of the bad, learn from it, and focus on the next play. This is very similar to 'flush it,' but 'park it' means

Culture Defeats Strategy 2 - Goonville, Texas Pop. 11

we want to come back to the mistake later and grow from it (one of our best call backs is 'failure is...growth!).

Steve Jones, head coach for the Kimberly Papermakers in Kimberly, Wisconsin, explained this concept to me. "We all drive a vehicle to work each day. We get out of it, go to work and then get back in it and go home. This is how we want to think about a mistake; when it happens, we stay at work. When work is over we then go back to it to go home or learn from it."

Every position group has their own way to physically release a mistake and park it.

For example: clap hands, snap fingers, 'wipe it off' (wipe top of numbers), roll hands, etc. After they make their physical release, they then take a deep breath. Oxygen is the magical healer for the brain. When we take a deep breath and exhale, it's a trigger for 'let it go'.

Demonstrating a physical release and deep breath after a mistake is tough to train them to do. It's rare when we see it but sure feels good to spot a corner across the field 'wiping it off' after he gives up a completion. Your coaches must constantly remind them in practice for a physical release or it won't be overlearned. Another great time to do this is in film review after practice. Our coaches will require athletes to 'shake it off' or whatever their routine is when they make a mistake on film.

"THEY AIN'T GIVING ANY SECOND-PLACE TROPHIES IN CUBA"

Yoel Romero is an Olympic medal-winning wrestler from Cuba (2000). Romero defected to Germany in 2007 and began his UFC career and was been very successful in that arena as well. In a podcast interview with Joe Rogan, (JRE MMA #17) Romero tells the fascinating Cuban model of training for wrestlers and other Olympic athletes.

"I've heard in Cuba the higher up you are the better you live in the Olympic Center. Is that true?", Rogan asked. Romero explains, "I have gone to Olympic centers all over the world. At each one, athlete #5 and #6 eat the same as #1. In Cuba, it's not like that. If you are ranked #3 you don't eat what #1 eats... #2 doesn't either,"

"The #1 guy has the most privileges. It's good and bad. It pushes you to be #1, but it is bad because all can't be the best at what they're doing," Romero says. "Cuba is small and has so many great performers so it must be very effective," Rogan asks. The interpreter, Joey Diaz, interjects, "they ain't giving any second-place trophies in Cuba!"

Romero says, "You don't want the trophies. You want to eat what the best guys eat and sit where the best guys sit. The guy who trains the most is the best."

"I lived in the Olympic Center 15 years. I lived with 10 guys who wanted to kill me the whole time. You have to become a machine mentally. Not only a machine when you fight, but in your life. The others can see when you're sick, when you have an injury or whatever. You live with them and they know everything. There are lots of rooms and guys from different cities in Cuba. You have to be a machine inside and out. Guys from the same cities will spy for each other so even the ones not in your weight class could be a spy against you. You always have spies watching you. I lived like this from 1995 - 2007."

Practice should mean something. There should be winners and losers for drills and team sessions. Our defensive players can earn a black jersey if they are one of our elite performers. This doesn't mean one of our 11 starters. They have to be 100% goon in every way. The classroom, effort, coachable, great teammate, etc.

Find ways to have your players earn incentives. Make them mean something and your practices will be more intense and your players will not feel the pressure as much on game day.

I covered a lot in this chapter. It was challenging to attempt to condense down the benefits of a well-organized, lots of repetition, intense practice that covers situations your players will face in games.

If you have a bunch of athletes like Tim Krumrie who can't wait to go all out in practice, then you can forget everything in this chapter and binge on Netflix immediately. If you live in the real world and have normal humans, you must make practice as game-like as possible. Great practices won't happen if we don't make them happen and we must always remember, practice is EVERYTHING.

CHAPTER 6 REVIEW
PRACTICE IS EVERYTHING

- Practice is learning a new skill. Training is perfecting the skill.

- Perfect training makes perfect. The 10,000-hour approach only makes sense if deliberate training is happening.

- Training sessions should be symphonies. It takes a lot effort by coaches beforehand for it to flow effortlessly.

- Practice to game ratio needed on a regular basis is 5:1.

- Repetition must have instant feedback so changes can be.

- Overlearning or muscle memory is built through myelin.

- Spaced repetition is speed up the learning process. Walk-through's are an excellent tool for this.

- Situations must be in your training plan. If it happens in a game it must be worked.

- Pressure is mandatory. There aren't any second-place trophies in Cuba.

CHAPTER 7
LESSON #6 – THE ELITE COACHING STAFF

> *"I absolutely believe that people, unless coached, never reach their maximum capabilities."*
>
> **Bob Nardelli**
> **CEO - The Home Depot**

"Coach Jackson, we are getting the supplies donated to install a sprinkler system on our practice field. We need to get it done as soon as possible when school is out." John Ferguson, who will go on my 'Mount Rushmore of administrators' when I retire, mentioned this to me shortly after I began my head coaching career at the before mentioned Paducah High School. What? I had been on the job for just a few weeks when I was told our staff of FOUR coaches needed to totally put in a sprinkler system. I grew up in a small town and had to do manual labor throughout my junior high and high school years, but I had zero idea how to install an underground sprinkler system.

We're talking about laying out where the sprinkler heads had to go, where the electricity had to be run to power them, using a trencher to dig the soil, laying PVC pipe, wiring the system, you name it. I was told, "if we have a free sprinkler system given to us, we have to get it in the ground."

Not only did I have to help figure this out, but had to motivate three guys who weren't starting their head

Culture Defeats Strategy 2 - Goonville, Texas Pop. 11

coaching career and weren't as excited as I was. After a few weeks and the two vocational agriculture teachers saving us with their knowledge of 'purple cleaner, glue, insert and turn' we finally got it installed. This was 'other duties assigned' in everyone's contract. No one got paid a dime for this. It was part of being a coach at Paducah High School.

What is a coach? It's a term often used but very few really know the origin of the word. 'Coach' came from 1400's Hungary in the village of Kocs. "An unknown carriage-maker in Kocs devised a larger, more comfortable carriage than any known at the time. It was called the Koczi szeter, a 'wagon of Kocs,' which was shortened to 'kocsi'," according to historian Robert Hendrickson.

Over time the larger kocsi cart became popular and was copied throughout Europe. In Germany, it was called a 'kutsche,' — 'coche' in France, and a 'coach' in England.

When our great country was being settled, travelers hired stagecoaches to safely get them from Point A to Point B. Oftentimes the journey was through dangerous territory. A journey they could not make without a coach to get them there.

Merriam Webster defines a coach as:

1. a. a large, usually closed four-wheeled horse-drawn carriage having doors on the sides and an elevated seat in front for the driver.

@CoachJacksonTPW   #culturematters

b. a railroad passenger car intended primarily for day travel.

2. a. a private tutor hired as a *coach* to help her daughter prepare for the test.
b. one who instructs or trains; *especially* one who instructs players in the fundamentals of a sport and directs team strategy.

Everyone's a coach and everything has a scoreboard. Most reading this book are an athletic coach but anyone who is a manager, teacher or leader of any kind are helping people get from Point A to Point B.

ELITE COACHES HAVE A GROWTH MINDSET

Gordon Wood was a legendary Texas high school coach who won 396 games in 43 seasons. His teams won or shared 25 district championships and nine state championships. Most of his time was spent (1960-1985) in Brownwood where they amassed seven AAA state championships.

In the article, 'Parcells Old Texas Inspiration', written by William Rhoden, Bill Parcells once credited Coach Wood with being an inspiration to him.

Parcells was the defensive coordinator at Texas Tech University in the spring of 1977 when he kept noticing, "a rough looking, leathery kind of looking guy wearing a maroon jacket and a 'B' on his cap. The man came back, and came back, and came back."

Culture Defeats Strategy 2 - Goonville, Texas Pop. 11

"We had 20 spring practices," Parcells said. *"I know he was there at least 15 times, always down by the linebackers."* Parcells finally introduced himself to Wood, who said he coached in *"a little town down the road from here."*

"Outside of Lubbock?" Parcells asked.

"No, a little further," Wood replied. *"I said, how far is it?"* Parcells recalled.

"Well, it's two and a half hours one way," Wood replied.

Parcells asked Wood if he stayed in a hotel, and Wood said no, he would drive up in the morning, watch practice then drive back home. Five hours on the road.

"And I know he did it least 15 times, and at the time he had to be 60 years old," Parcells recalled.

Wood was actually 63. At the end of spring practice, Wood told Parcells he'd been watching him and thought he was pretty good. Then he peppered him with questions. *"He asked, 'Why you are teaching this?, show me how you do that,' "* Parcells said. *"Here's a guy who never lost, he never ever lost. I think of him every season when we start. I think about this guy."*

Another amazing story of Coach Wood being obsessed with learning was told by former Baylor head coach Grant Teaff. "One Sunday morning I came in after a game and I noticed someone sleeping on a small couch in our film room. It was Coach Wood. He had spent the night in there so he could ask me a question about a particular play we had run during the game. What makes it even more amazing is Coach Wood was RETIRED at the time."

I started my coaching career in 1990. In the spring of 1991 I heard Coach Wood speak at a clinic in Mineral Wells, Texas. He was 76 years old. He had been retired for six years but was still active in the profession and investing in the next generation.

At the end of his presentation, Coach Wood implored the audience to support the coaching fraternity more. "The coaching profession doesn't take care of each other enough. We have people in our communities everywhere shooting arrows at us, criticizing every third down call and second-guessing who we play at quarterback. We need to support each other when we can. Here is how I still do it even in retirement; when I stop for gas in another town I always ask the cashier, 'who is the head football coach here?' He or she will give me the name and then I always say, 'oh yea, I know him. What a great man and coach. Y'all are lucky to have him running the program here.' Every time the cashier stands just a little taller. I can tell they are proud their coach has been complimented. I think they tell the next few locals who come in someone says they are lucky to have their coach. It takes one minute and it is the right thing to do. I challenge you guys to find ways like this to take care of each other when you can. Our profession deserves it."

> *"Leadership and learning are indispensable to each other."*
>
> John F. Kennedy

LEADERS ARE LEARNERS

Carol Dweck coined the phrase 'growth mindset' in her 2006 book, "Mindset." Dweck's research led her to conclude there are two general mindsets people hold when it comes to dealing with change and growth: either a fixed mindset or a growth mindset.

If you do not have an obsessed desire to learn you are hurting those you coach. Gordon Wood couldn't stop learning even after he retired. Those with growth mindsets push themselves to improve something because they do not want to remain stagnant or unsuccessful.

Bobby Hurley Sr. is considered one of the top high school basketball coaches ever. He is one of only three high school coaches inducted into the Naismith Basketball Hall of Fame and has won an ESPN 'ESPY.' His teams at St. Anthony's in Jersey City, New Jersey won 28 state basketball championships, 1,184 games and he has coached over 150 Division 1 players. His secret to success? "Don't own a set of golf clubs. When I go to a clinic, I go to every session. I don't go half a day and play golf half a day." Coach Hurley has a room in his house dedicated just for clinic notebooks.

High achievers have a growth mindset. One of the easiest ways to grow is to read. You are paid to read if you are a leader of any type. Embarrassingly, I used to sort of brag about not ever reading, but not anymore. I now realize people who are 'crushing it' in their fields are readers. John Wooden's dad, Joshua, told him to "drink deeply from good books."

The more you read the more confidence you will get by learning from others. Dr. Gilbert of the Success Hotline, says, "some people act like they are paid to watch TV. They watch 30-40 hours of TV a week. It's like a full-time job." I have certainly been guilty of watching too much TV in my life. I am sure Greg Popovich doesn't keep up with Game of Thrones or any other television series. High achievers pay the price with being committed to learning.

Benefits of reading:

- Your vocabulary will increase. Vocabulary is the #1 indicator of knowledge.

- When you read to learn with a growth mindset it challenges your current thinking or confirms what you already believe. Just because you were taught something years ago or have believed in a certain way to do things doesn't make it right. Words that kill any organization: 'we've always done it this way.'

- Reading provides new ideas or a different perspective. When I read I always take notes and most of the time new ideas will spawn from something I read.

- Relieve stress. Reading is a great way to relax. Studies have shown that reading for six minutes can reduce stress by 84%.

> *"Not all readers are leaders, but all leaders are readers."*
>
> Harry S. Truman
> 33rd President of the United States

Culture Defeats Strategy 2 - Goonville, Texas Pop. 11

- Bill Belichick believes he may have the greatest football library in the world.

- Bill Gates reads 50 books a year.

- Mark Zuckerberg reads at least one book every two weeks.

- Warren Buffett reads six hours each day.

- Mark Cuban reads for more than three hours every day.
- Elon Musk grew up reading two books a day, according to his brother.

- Arthur Blank, cofounder of Home Depot, reads two hours a day.

- Phil Knight, founder of Nike, has an extraordinary home library. If he allows you to see it you must take off your shoes and bow before entering.

Author Tom Corley spent five years studying the habits of 233 rich people and 128 poor people. He published the results in the article, 'Rich Habits: The Daily Success Habits of Wealthy Individuals'. One of the most telling differences is the amount of television watched between the two groups. 67% of rich people limit their T.V. to one hour or less a day, compared to only 23% of poor people.

BOOKS ALL LEADERS OR COACHES SHOULD READ

Above The Line - Urban Meyer

Chop Wood Carry Water - Joshua Medcalf

David and Goliath - Malcolm Gladwell

Extreme Ownership - Jocko Willink and Leif Babin

Generation iY - Tim Elmore

Grit - Angela Duckworth

It's Your Ship - Michael Abrashoff

Leaders Eat Last - Simon Sinek

Legacy - James Kerr

Outliers - Malcolm Gladwell

The 12 Pillars of Peak Performance - Brian Cain

The Captain Class - Sam Walker

The Slight Edge - Jeff Olsen

The Talent Code - Daniel Coyle

Win Forever - Pete Carroll

You Win in the Locker Room First - Jon Gordon and Mike Smith

Erik Bakich, the head baseball coach at the University of Michigan, says he reads a book a week. I can't read a book a week just like you probably can't. One way to get 'some book knowledge' is to let Brian Johnson read them for you. Brian Johnson's Philosopher's Notes is an outstanding way to get the main ideas of a book in a fifteen-minute video he produces. I will watch a video of a book once a day for five days and take notes each time. By the end of the fifth day I have it stored in my brain pretty well.

> *"If your vehicle is only moving your body, you are missing its full potential."*
>
> — Skip Prichard

AUTOMOBILE UNIVERSITY

Another great way to grow is to turn off the radio in your car. The late motivational speaker and author, Zig Ziglar, coined the phrase "automobile university," to refer to the use of the time spent behind the wheel to expand one's education. He suggested that many drivers can increase their knowledge about a variety of subjects quite a lot during their drive time. "If you live in a metropolitan and drive 12,000 miles a year, in three years' time you can acquire the equivalent of two years of college education. It ought to be the greatest educational institution in the world."

Try listening to a few podcasts as you are driving. 'Auto U,' has been a 'game changer' for me when I had a long commute and when I have traveled to speak at clinics or seminars.

SUCCESS HOTLINE

Each day I listen to Dr. Rob Gilbert's Success Hotline (973-743-4690). Dr. Gilbert produces a three-minute audio recording each morning that focuses on becoming a better you. It has become a terrific part of my routine. I will record some of his messages and our team will listen to it as part of our Leadership Academy.

PODCASTS

Until I met Brian Cain in 2015, I didn't know what podcasts really were. They are a tremendous way to listen to any subject you are interested in. You can subscribe to your favorite which will be downloaded to your device for you to listen to at your convenience (working out of 'Auto U').

Great leadership podcasts I listen to

Finding Mastery - Michael Gervais

Focus 3 - Tim and Brian Kight

Hardcore History - Dan Carlin

Inside the Headset - AFCA

Jocko Podcast - Jocko Willink

Lead with a Story Podcast - Paul Smith

Leading the Next Generation - Tim Elmore

The Culture Classroom - John Torrey and John Weaver

Optimize - Brian Johnson

TED Radio Hour - NPR

The Learning Leader Show - Ryan Hawk

The Mackey Speaks Leadership Podcast - Stephen Mackey

The Joe Rogan Experience - Joe Rogan

USA Football Coach and Coordinator Podcast - USA Football

Culture Defeats Strategy 2 - Goonville, Texas Pop. 11

Just like my book list on the previous page, this is a really tough list to put out there. I'm 100% positive I have forgotten to include a few.

YOUTUBE

Matt Rhule, head football coach for the Carolina Panthers, sent me a link for a YouTube video of Greg Popovich speaking to basketball coaches in Berlin. He told me he usually listens to a clinic as he falls asleep each night. I responded by telling him about the Success Hotline. He replied, 'very cool, I'm on it.' Great coaches are constantly learning.

I remember the days we made VHS tapes to give to college coaches to help our players with recruitment. Then, DVDs came along and all of us were excited they didn't take up so much space. Now, everything is online for college coaches to view. They can watch seconds after hanging up the phone with a high school coach to determine if a player fits their mold.

Learning has also evolved for coaches. There is so much knowledge online for free if we would just turn off the TV and access it. I used to think YouTube was for bored people to watch mindless hours of useless stuff. I love a good cat video as much as the next guy, but YouTube is the place to watch recordings of experts in every field imaginable teach others.

YouTube has been called 'A classroom in your pocket' and I agree. You can search 'coaching clinic,' 'volleyball coaching' or anything related to your field and hundreds of videos will pop up.

Julius Yego - "Mr. YouTube Man"

Julius Yego grew up poor in rural Kenya. He came from a family of farmers, a home without electricity and had to walk six miles to school. Somehow, in a country known for distance runners, Julius fell in love with the javelin. He had no money for one so he made 'stick javelins' and threw every day growing up. "My dad did not want me throwing the javelin. He was worried it would hinder my studies. I used to not tell him when I was going to competitions."

"Nowhere in Kenya was there javelin training. I didn't have a coach. I was training alone, I saw it as life was going against me. It was the lowest point in my life."

"But I didn't give up. First time I was on YouTube is 2009, when I was now getting serious about training and I didn't have a coach," he explained. "Nobody was there for me to see if I was doing well or not, so I went to the cyber cafe. I would see what the champion throwers would do in their normal training. I would go practice it the next day. Eventually, I got teammates to train with me but we still did not have a coach."

Yego's cyber café training started paying off in a big way. At the 2011 All-Africa Games, Yego became the first Kenyan to win a title in a field event. When journalists wanted to interview Yego's coach, the secret of his success was revealed.

Culture Defeats Strategy 2 - Goonville, Texas Pop. 11

"They wanted to interview my coach to know what I did before the competitions, the championships. But I told them seriously I didn't have a coach. I didn't go with a coach," he said. "Then they asked me, 'Who is your coach,' and then I told them, 'YouTube.'"

By 2015 Yego, with the help of coaching finally, became the first Kenyan to ever win a World Championship in a field event. He was a silver medalist at the 2016 Olympics in Rio de Janeiro. "My son likes javelin, I promise he won't go without a coach," Yego said.

If a poor kid in Kenya who grew up without electricity can go to a small cyber café, watch free videos on YouTube and learn how to become a world-class javelin-thrower, what is our excuse? If you're a running back coach, get on YouTube and see what's out there. Maybe there is one or two things you can learn to help your players. If you are a teacher the same is true.

In 1990, Quinlan-Ford High School gave me a set of keys and a teacher's edition. I had only done my student-teaching in middle school P.E. so I w as a little intimidated. Now, I could use YouTube to watch master health teachers across the world teach lessons.

> *"There are two equalizers in life — the internet and education."*
>
> **John Chambers**
> **Chairman and CEO**
> **Cisco Corporation**

TED TALKS

TED Talks (Technology, Entertainment and Design) are conferences held throughout North America, Europe and Asia. The speakers are given a maximum of 18 minutes to present their ideas in the most innovative and engaging ways they can. They address a wide range of topics within the research and practice of science and culture, often through storytelling.

In 2006, attendance cost was $4,400 per person and was by invitation only. The membership model was shifted in January 2007 to an annual membership fee of $6,000, which includes attendance of the conference, club mailings, networking tools, and conference DVDs. The 2018 conference was $10,000 per attendee. Why care how much it cost to attend the conference (now in Vancouver, BC)? None of us should because we can watch them for free online. The TED website has over 2,600 presentations available and of course, YouTube has thousands as well.

ELITE COACHES ARE PHYSICALLY FIT

In the article, The Way of the Monastic Warrior: Lessons from Major Dick Winters, written by Brett and Kate McKay, they describe how committed Major Winters was to physical fitness. *Winters kept up his exercise habit even after Easy Company deployed for combat missions, finding it invaluable in mitigating the stress that accumulated from having to regularly make life and death decisions. He committed himself to a rigorous routine, in which "there were only a few days that I didn't run two or three miles, do 80 push-ups, 60*

Culture Defeats Strategy 2 - Goonville, Texas Pop. 11

sit-ups on a foot locker, a couple of splits, and some leg and trunk exercises after the day's work was over."

> **"To have long-term success as a coach or in any position of leadership you have to be obsessed in some way."**
>
> **Pat Riley**
> **President, Miami Heat**

Winters felt that it was his training that ultimately allowed him to remain mentally alert, control his fear, and avoid breaking down under stress.

"Because I was in such good shape, my fatigue level never reached the point of physical exhaustion that contributes to mental exhaustion and, ultimately, to combat fatigue. We all experienced sleep deprivation at times-that is the nature of stress-but a physically exhausted leader routinely makes poor decisions in a time of crisis."

Are you hearing this, coaches? Please don't think I'm comparing our stress with combat stress. I would never insult the brave men and women who deal with it, but we do have stress.

I use the term 'getting in the submarine' when football season starts. It's like we go under the water and don't come out again for months. We love it and wouldn't trade it but that doesn't mean we shouldn't see the benefits of getting in shape for the season and remaining that way during the season.

Without a doubt, the most quoted, and I guess controversial or at the least hurt some people's feelings, from CDS 1 was 'great leaders aren't fat.' I certainly didn't mean to offend others but I wanted to give them the same real talk Brian Cain gave me. It was the wake-up call I needed. More importantly, I'm a better coach and leader because I'm 30 pounds lighter.

It's not about sitting in front of a monitor and watching Hudl for hours on end. We are better leaders when we take care of ourselves.

Sweat 30 minutes a day

The brain releases 'feel-good' chemicals when we sweat for 30 minutes. It doesn't matter how we do it but it needs to happen. Endorphins interact with receptors in our brain that not only trigger a positive feeling in the body, but reduces the perception of pain.

Studies show it only takes 30 minutes of moderate exercise (that creates a sweat) for us to get multiple benefits:
- heart health
- weight loss
- stress reducer
- mood booster
- energy burst
- improve memory

Get a System to Sweat

Going to the weight room and then figuring out what you are going to do is not going to get much done. My system is having someone work me out at Orange Theory Fitness whenever possible. I don't have to plan anything, I just have to show up. Classes are up to 24 'orange athletes' at a time with one coach leading us through a 60-minute workout. Approximately half is on the treadmill and the other half is on a water rower, using dumb bells, TRX straps, etc. If there isn't an OTF near you or this isn't a great option, there are many apps that work similarly. I used to get cardio type workouts on YouTube and follow along.

I know you can read lots of other books (or listen to podcasts) if you are interested in learning more about exercising so I won't spend any more time on it here. But, if you want to be an elite coach the research is staring you in the face-sweating 30-minutes a day is part of the equation. If you already have a routine of fitness you are shaking your head 'yes' right now. If you aren't in a habit of working out, trust me and try it for five days. You will get addicted to the endorphin rush and your team will get a better coach.

THE ASSISTANT COACH FROM HEAVEN

I wasn't an elite assistant coach. I was a good one who had ambition to move up, but looking back there are lots of things I wish I could go back and do different.

Coach Neighbors, writes a great blog even during his women's basketball season. In one of them he talks about what makes a great assistant coach. He uses the comparison of an assistant

Culture Defeats Strategy 2 - Goonville, Texas Pop. 11

coach with Leo McGarry (pictured) the fictional television character on the series 'The West Wing.'

Coach Neighbors writes, '*McGarry was portrayed by the late John Spencer as the President's Chief of Staff. Throughout the six-season run, Leo was at the right hand of the President of the United States (the POTUS for you West Wingers). He was in the office every morning before the POTUS. He was in the office until the POTUS left for the day. He coordinated the daily functions of the office. He never let a problem get past his office to the oval office. He provided the POTUS with input when asked. He had ideas of his own, most of which were never used, but never was off message with the message of the POTUS. He literally took a bullet for the POTUS and figuratively on many more occasions. And on most days, no one ever knew who he was. In other words, Leo McGarry was the ultimate ASSISTANT COACH.*

Coach Neighbors hit this one right on the head. If I could go back in time (or if I'm ever one again), I would be a better assistant coach. I would be more like Leo McGarry.

A. THE ELITE ASSISTANT UNDERSTANDS LOYALTY

Loyalty – a strong feeling of support or allegiance.

I asked on Twitter for suggestions to include in this chapter on coaching, and loyalty was by far the #1 suggestion. Loyalty is another word that is said often but not defined much. In my Culture Factory presentations, I say culture is tough to define but everyone knows it when they see it. Loyalty is the same way.

Culture Defeats Strategy 2 - Goonville, Texas Pop. 11

> *"My loyalty to Country and Team is beyond reproach."*
>
> **Navy SEAL Creed**

In coaching, there are a lot of ways to 'skin a cat' so to speak. There can and should be lots of discussion in the coaches' office about how to attack a certain defense or player but loyalty is 'one voice' outside the office. In fact, I say to our staff you should sell it to your unit group so enthusiastically they might think it was your idea. If a coach says to his players, "This is Coach Jackson's idea that we settled on after a long discussion. It's a little different than we have done but maybe it'll be fine." Every player in the room can feel the skepticism which is also disloyalty.

How you speak at all times is another indicator of loyalty. Silence is not loyalty either. If you are at the barber shop and someone says, "What was Coach Jackson thinking when he onside kicked to start the second half? Good Lord, he needs to trust his defense a little bit." If you say, "I'm not sure, you better ask him." Disloyal. Support him by saying that it's a program philosophy all coaches agree with. If it drives you crazy go find another school where the head coach kicks it deep every time.

Loyalty is not just to the head coach but to each other. In the Navy SEAL training program, instructors from day one preaches that their team is everything. You succeed with them, and you fail without them. Lastly, you never leave anyone behind.

People who like to gossip, slander and are just highly critical openly, without reserve, are not loyal. The

Culture Defeats Strategy 2 - Goonville, Texas Pop. 11

world is tough on coaches. An elite staff can't have even one coach who delights in negative talk on another coach.

Loyalty is a two-way street. Head coaches have to strive to create a climate where everyone is allowed to be involved in the decision making. 'Guilty as charged' that I have been too 'it has to be this way' at times. I still have 'close-fisted' things I believe in and won't compromise on but I have also relaxed a little on things where there can be some flexibility (everything matters so this is tough!).

Steve Bragg, now retired athletic director for Mesquite I.S.D. in Mesquite, Texas, told me one time when I was the head coach at Mesquite Poteet, "You don't really know someone until you go through the fire with them."

Tim Krause, is author of the book, 'Touching Hearts - Teaching Greatness.' In it, he tells the story of a head coach who called a timeout at the end of a game to set up a game-winning play. *His assistant coach came up with a strategy the head coach felt would work. So, the decision was made to go with the assistant's suggestion. When the play was run – it completely backfired and the game was lost. After the game, a group of disgruntled fans asked, "Who was responsible for that last play?" With his assistant at his side, the head coach answered, "Me." In that moment, the head coach gained the loyalty and respect of not only his assistant but also the players.'*

Loyalty is the most important trait. Loyalty to the head coach and to each other. Have one enthusiastic voice as long as you are on the staff. If or when you realize you can't do it this way it is much better to find a new position than to be disloyal.

> *"If you work for a man, in heaven's name work for him, speak well of him, and stand by the institution he represents. Remember, an ounce of loyalty is worth a pound of cleverness. If you must growl, condemn, and eternally find fault-resign your position, and when you are on the outside, damn to your heart's content – but as long as you are part of the institution, do not condemn it. If you do, the first high wind that comes along will blow you away, and probably you will never know why."*
>
> Elbert Hubbard

B. THE ELITE ASSISTANT IS BLUE COLLAR AND WILL PICK UP A BROOM

I was fortunate enough to speak at the Nike Clinic in Portland in 2018. Dabo Swinney was one of the keynote speakers. Before he really got into his presentation on receiver play he gave this nugget to coaches just getting started. "Young coaches put your head down and stay patient. I was at the AFCA convention waiting at the elevator to go to my room and a young coach asked me, 'what is one thing I can do to move up the ladder as a coach?' 'Son, I am about to get in this elevator and punch the button for the 14th floor. I have earned the right to do this, but you need to go to the stairwell and take the stairs'," Coach Swinney replied to him.

Culture Defeats Strategy 2 - Goonville, Texas Pop. 11

We wash, dry and put our goon's workout gear in a locker for them every day. This is a major job that is never ending. We have done this job different ways over the years, but this year at NF three coaches volunteered to take care of it.

Michael Ludlow and Ryan Porter are our laundry duty coaches. Both are responsible for game-planning, practice scripts, assistant coaches on their side of the ball and a plethora of other things that going into being a coordinator. I tell both them they are the 'head coach of the offense/defense'.

Neither of these guys were handed a duty roster that had their name on laundry. Their attitude was, 'this is important so let us do it by ourselves. It will get done correctly every day.'

When I got into coaching I was afraid to begin in a big district in their middle school feeder system. I was worried it would take me years to move up the ranks to become a freshman coach and then a varsity coach. I just assumed everyone wanted to be a head coach and had that type of ambition. Some do and some don't and there is nothing wrong with coaches who serve the middle school staffs for their career. In fact, I tip my cap to them. Guys who teach the fundamentals and more importantly teach the love of the game in football, basketball and track are some of the most important coaches in any program.

Young coaches, don't be afraid to take the stairs. It is not that hard to outwork most coaches who are not driven or straining to move up the ladder. Every year I tell the middle school coaches in the systems that feed our high school this, "if you want to move up you must do more than is expected. Please don't come to me in the spring and tell me how bad you want to be at the high school when you haven't come up any on Saturday during football season, haven't volunteered to officiate our powerlifting meet, haven't helped us officiate 7 v. 7, etc."

It doesn't work like that. Every head coach of every sport reading this book loves it when a young coach who 'gets it' joins their staff. A young coach who works their tail off and is always asking 'what's next.'

C. ELITE COACHES SEE MORE THAN AVERAGE COACHES

There is a big different between merely watching something and observing with intent. I am what some people call 'conservative' with my money. Casinos build those huge complexes with money they make on 'games of chance' that are all slightly tilted in their favor.

Casinos spend a lot of money on surveillance to protect the business. Derek Boss and Alan Zajic wrote the book, 'Casino Security and Gaming Surveillance' and in it they describe what must happen to protect the casino.

"Casino surveillance is to protect the business. We must deliberately observe and not just 'watch.' Most new surveillance operators are not trained in the technique of proper patrol. Most, in fact, are trained to patrol randomly and not in a systematic manner. It is important to remember that 'a random patrol equals random results!' Random results will cost your casino money, a loss of efficiency, and will not deter crime. Surveillance management should operate under the

Culture Defeats Strategy 2 - Goonville, Texas Pop. 11

premise that crime is occurring somewhere within the casino or on the property each and every shift, every day. Why? Because it's true."

This is a tough analogy, but most coaches are not trained to intentionally observe. There is constant time for coaches to see, evaluate and give feedback. I have had coaches say to me, "I didn't notice John needed to shave." "I just don't see them walking to the drills because I am looking at my practice schedule." Not ok. Elite coaches see everything.

Pete Carroll talks about one of the lessons he learned from Bud Grant was to 'always be watching.' In Carroll's book, Win Forever (greatness), he recalls how Coach Grant influenced him to use his peripheral vision so to speak and broaden his field as vision so he could observe his players at every opportunity. *'He taught me that if you learn to become a good watcher and listener, you'll be rewarded with a wealth of information that you can use to compete more successfully. I learned from him that the best teachers, coaches, and leaders are often the best observers. Watching and particular, listening, intently is critical.'*
'I remember one occasion in particular when I was the defensive backs coach at the Vikings and Bud was head coach. It was the very first day of fall camp, and Bud had sent the players out on a long-distance run circling the field. For most coaches - including me at the time - that would have been a chance for some downtime, and that's how we were treating it. I recall standing on the edge of the field jabbering with one of my fellow coaches, when I saw Coach Grant glaring at me. "Pete! What the hell is the matter with you?" he snapped. "You're not watching!"

@CoachJacksonTPW　　#culturematters

Culture Defeats Strategy 2 - Goonville, Texas Pop. 11

Coach Carroll goes on to say how Coach Grant used the simple exercise as an open book; who was out in front, who stayed in the cluster, who slowed down or sped up relative to their positions and the rest of the group. Coach Grant didn't have them running to get them in shape as much as put them a situation where he could observe their competitive natures.

Tim and Brian Kight on their Focus 3 podcast say, 'great coaches are master observers. They see more than other coaches. Not only do they observe scheme and technique, they see everything.'

To see everything, you must place yourself in the correct area of the field. You can't stand in the middle of a drill and see every athlete working. This seems to be the default location for most coaches when running a drill. See them all to coach them all. Stand at a 45 degree angle off to one side so you can observe each repetition. For example, when four athletes are performing the power clean all four of them deserve for their lift to be witnessed and get either correction or a 'atta boy'. When things get hard they know if you are not watching them. The non-Krumrie athletes will skip a rep when he or she realizes no one is watching.

Early in my career I remember riding back on 'yellow dog' buses after football games and track meets. Some coaches could never hear foul language in the back of the bus. Some would put their head down and be asleep or pretend to be asleep so they didn't have to deal with anything. Everything matters! Every player on every bus knows which coach will let things slide and which won't. Don't be that coach who doesn't see much.

Observing is intentionality. If it is important to you, coach it. Be intentional and look for it.

D. ELITE COACHES ARE TRUTH TELLERS AND DON'T AVOID CONFLICT

"Male teachers, if there is a fight in the hallway don't wait on the coaches to stop it and take care of it. If you don't have it in you to bow your neck and separate two of our students you may need to get out of education." Another principal 'hero' I have had the pleasure to serve with made this statement. Steve Steadham was an interim principal Lone Oak High School when he made this edict in a faculty meeting. I couldn't agree more then or now. You shouldn't be in education in any capacity or in a leadership position if you are a conflict-avoider.

I ask lots of college recruiters when they come by, "What is the #1 thing your program does to develop toughness?" Trey Haverty, secondary coach at SMU, gave me a great response in the spring of 2019. "Coaches must be willing to deal with confrontation when it is necessary. Coach Dykes and our staff are constantly holding players accountable. If someone loafs on film we will confront it head-on in a meeting with the entire team present. We don't tear them down, but they aren't afraid of calling them out when necessary."

In the article, Ferguson's Formula, by Anita Elberse, Sir Alex Ferguson explains his view of having control of the team and not allowing 'the stars' of Manchester United to influence the culture. *"You can't ever lose control—not when you are dealing with 30 top professionals who are all millionaires,"* Ferguson told us. *"And if any players want to take me on, to challenge my authority and control, I deal with them."*

Coach Ferguson is also going to wait to deal with issues. *"If someone has failed to meet expectations, don't wait to correct them. I would do it right after the game. I wouldn't wait until Monday. I'd do it, and it was finished. I was on to the next match."*

"For a player—for any human being—there is nothing better than hearing "Well done." Those are the two best words ever invented. You don't need to use superlatives."

"At the same time, in the dressing room, you need to point out mistakes when players don't meet expectations. That is when reprimands are important. I would do it right after the game. I wouldn't wait until Monday. I'd do it, and it was finished. I was on to the next match. There is no point in criticizing a player forever."

Bill Parcells was always known as a truth-teller. "You have to be honest with people — brutally honest. You have to tell them the truth about their performance, you have to tell it to them face-to-face, and you have to tell it to them over and over again. Sometimes the truth will be painful, and sometimes saying it will lead to an uncomfortable confrontation. So be it. The only way to change people is to tell them in the clearest possible terms what they're doing wrong. And if they don't want to listen, they don't belong on the team."

Chapter 4 is titled 'Help Raise Them.' We are a relationship-based program but you can't raise your own children if you are a conflict-avoider. There are teachers across the country who have to deal with

@CoachJacksonTPW   #culturematters

children of parents who avoid confrontation. It makes their job harder on a daily basis.

I have heard more than once, "some of our teachers here are afraid of some of the students. They won't send them to get a tardy slip or tell them to take off their headphones." What? Steve Steadham can't be everywhere. All kids deserve to have all their teachers and coaches 'bow their neck' and take care of what needs taking care of.

With experience comes wisdom. I am better now at knowing when not to confront, when to confront, and where it should happen. I do know this, if we had not some 'come to Jesus' confrontations after it became 'their fault', the 2018 seniors would have graduated without the season they deserved. I am passionate about this subject. I wrote in CDS 1, 'changing a culture is not for the faint of heart.' If you are going to look the other way on the little things and avoid conflict you will get the culture you deserve. The 90% of your team who is in the wheelbarrow won't get the culture they deserve.

"Must be nice. Eleven offers, they'll see." In 2017 one of our senior receivers, a three-year starter with multiple scholarship offers, made this statement to our head trainer at the time, Holly Abshire. We were finishing up a convincing win in the fourth quarter to take our record to 3-0. A young 'goon' had just caught a short pass and it didn't sit well with one of our better players. Wait, what? He was mad because he hadn't caught as many passes as he would have liked but he was also telling a member of our staff?

Culture Defeats Strategy 2 - Goonville, Texas Pop. 11

I didn't hear about the comment until our staff meeting after the game. I was livid. Coach Wallis, one of our receiver coaches, told me, "Don't worry about it, boss. I will address it with him severely tomorrow morning."

I knew he would do a great job of getting his point across in private but I also wanted it addressed in our team meeting after weights. Our routine is consistent on these meetings. We start with kicking film, stats, what we did well and what we need to improve on. But, this week it was time to address the culture of 'me' from the night before.

"Guys, we have worked our butts off to be 3-0. I know you are tired of being 'the other team in Forney' and we are making strides, but something was said last night on the sidelines I can't live with," I said to them. "Coach Wallis asked me if he could say something (he rarely addressed the entire team) to everyone. I am in agreement we need some real talk in here today so I appreciate him wanting to speak."

Coach Wallis is demanding but in an 'arm-around, off to the side' sort of way. For him to express anger to the group I knew would be powerful. "Last night was the most disappointing thing I can remember from my career. Some of y'all would rather go 2-8 with a ton of selfish touches then go 8-2 and spread the ball around if that's what works best for the team. I've never seen anything like it."

Lots of coaches would have said, 'He's a senior. Let's get through the season and change the attitudes with the younger guys in the offseason.' That would be wrong. This group deserved better and this young man deserved better. This was one of those watershed moments that helped change our team for the better. The conflict needed to happen or we would have lost more of the control we had worked so hard to get since February.

> *"Your beliefs become your thoughts. Your thoughts become your words. Your words become your actions. Your actions become your habits. Your habits become your values. Your values become your destiny."*
>
> **Mahatma Ghandi**

E. ELITE COACHES HAVE THEIR OWN CORE VALUES

Tim Elmore, founder of Growing Leaders, in an interview with Ohio State Athletic Director Gene Smith, made this statement, "you hire the culture you want." "I agree," Coach Smith responded. He then talked about personal core values being the most important characteristic he is looking for when hiring someone to join the athletic department at OSU. "99% of the time their jaw drops when I ask them, what are four values you live by," Coach Smith said.

I have stolen this interview tactic from Coach Smith. I don't ask for four values but I normally end it with, "We are a core values program. Our values guide how we do things on a day to day basis. What would you say is the #1 core you live by?"

Tim Kight of FOCUS 3 says, "You can't lead others until you can lead yourself. We all need to be clear and deliberate about our personal core values. We should write them out our values and a credo for how we will live."

I challenge you to search yourself and think about what values are essential to you. What are 'close-fisted' values you will not compromise? What have been your three greatest accomplishments? What have been three events where you had to overcome adversity? Who are three mentors you have learned from and what values do they live by?

We have five daily core values at NF. This is a manageable number we can actually live out consistently as a program. I recommend the same for you. Write down four to five values you will use as a personal standard to live by. When we have the discipline to live with consistent behavior we will not only have more fulfillment but we have the right to lead others.

> **"It's not hard to make decisions when you know what your values are."**
> **Roy Disney**

Zappos CEO, Tony Hsieh, says "One of the really interesting things I found from the research is that it actually doesn't matter what your values are, what matters is that you have them. Our message is 'you should figure out what your personal core values are. If core values are pivotal to a company's conception, can pinpointing individual ones, help guide one's career? Can creating your own help you tune into the right job?"

F. MILLENNIAL COACHES - C'MON MAN

Millennials. Veteran coaches like me aren't sure sometimes about the generation iY (born between 1990-2000) coaches on our staffs. Most of the ones I have worked with are terrific. They are kid-magnets, eager, great teachers and will get better and better each year. But, others I have worked with seem a little entitled and want to be a coordinator before they are 25. I laid off the people who need to lose weight in this book so I guess I might as well offend some of the young guys.

Tim Elmore of Growing Leaders says that younger coaches are part of the generation that 'wants it now.' *'They've not heard the word "no" very often growing up. As a student or new employee, they expect to get their way and don't see why adults can't understand their perspective.'*

A couple of observations from a 30-year veteran that can help some of you who are just starting out:

- When you're given a job, take it as a compliment and attack it. Complete each assignment with a 'do more than is expected' attitude and you will be an invaluable member of the staff that your head coach won't want to live without.

- A polo shirt and khakis are for teaching class not for interviewing for a job.

Josh McCown is one of our receiver coaches NF. Josh is from east Texas and was relocating to the Dallas area so he was looking for a job. He sent me a resume and - although it looked great - I had lots of great applicants who were local so I wasn't sure if I was going to bring him in to interview.

A week or so went by and Josh just showed up unannounced wearing a sports coat and tie. He said, "I know I don't have an appointment but I was in the area so I wanted to drop off another resume, meet you and let you put a face with a name."

Advantage, McCown. This impressed me just like it would any head coach. He took the initiative to stop by and dressed up to do it. I set up an interview for him to meet our principal and he was hired shortly thereafter.

- Put your phone up. It is frustrating to be talking to a group of coaches and see the top of someone's head because they can't detach from their phone. Millennials are the most socially-connected generation in history but with the fewest number of personal friends. Most are computer experts, connected all over the world by email, instant messages, text messages, and the internet.

- Whatever is important to your head coach needs to be important to you. It's not hard to figure out what the 'close-fisted' beliefs of the program are from the top down. Ride for the brand.

- Dress like a professional. Nathan Stanley, athletic director for Lakewood ISD in Lakewood Oregon, tells a story of giving a young coach some direction on how to dress for practice. "We had a young coach in 2003 at Clackamas High School who I knew was going to be a good one. Early in the season he showed up for practice every day in flip-flops, hat on backward and a big gulp in his hand. I would always half-jokingly yell to him, "Nice professionalism." One day his dad heard it and something snapped so he ripped him about dressing like a coach should look. Today, he and I still joke about it. Sometimes when he sees me he will ask, "How's my professionalism today?"

- Get out of the coaches' office when athletes are present. There's not a lot to expound on this. There is a time to be in the coaches' office after practice but that time is not when athletes are in the locker room. Take this time to tell someone you don't coach how much you appreciate them.

- Be ok with coaching everybody. One of the best things we do at NF (and everywhere I've been) is have every football coach work with players on every team. On Thursday night, we play our sub-varsity games. Our freshman and junior varsity squads will play at opposite sites, so we have coaches going multiple places.

Justin Velasquez, our lead receiver coach, works with every receiver in our program grades 9-12. Our freshmen practice from 3:30-5:30 pm (our varsity and JV are in the mornings) so Coach Velasquez is with them when they are working offense. Every one of our coaches will do the same thing. None of them have too big of an ego to not coach the freshman and do it in an elite way.

Young coaches, when you learn how to coach the middle school athlete or the freshman who is just figuring out the basics it will make you a better coach. You will learn 'everything matters' and get a head start

Culture Defeats Strategy 2 - Goonville, Texas Pop. 11

on developing relationships with the future of the program.

- Get with a great staff and don't worry about your title. I was concerned about this way too much as a young coach. A coordinator from a losing program is not as enticing to hire as a position coach who has worked and learned in a solid program.

- If you coach at a smaller school where the coaches paint the field, you have to drive a bus, keep the clock at basketball games, etc. consider yourself lucky. You are learning how to work. Principals like Steve Steadham will value having you on their staff because you will not only 'bow your neck' when you need to but you aren't afraid to get your hands dirty.

'YES SIR, CONSIDER IT DONE.'

My mentor Phil Blue tells a great story about the answer always being 'yes.' He wrote about the experience in a great article titled, 'The Joys of Coaching in Small Schools' for Texas Coach Magazine.

In the spring of 2000, Farmersville High School in Farmersville, Texas was building a new football field. Coach Blue writes about a situation very similar to my sprinkler install at Paducah. *'I asked our superintendent, Joe Simpson, a question about the goal post installation and got this response, "You have a bunch of smart, young coaches, why don't y'all install them?" I said, "Yes sir, consider it done," and I proceeded to inform my staff of our new task ... JOY! As we surveyed the grass field, the obvious question became apparent, how do we know where to put the goal post? There are no markers, field lines, etc. We were just looking at a large field of grass inside a track.*

Our defensive coordinator, Todd Werts, who was also a math teacher, began to explain the initial plan for solving this puzzle. Jason Evans, another coach on staff, explained the steps for executing the plan. We purchased about six rolls of string and a bunch of stakes from the local hardware store. Two other assistants, Don Brown and Kevin Garvin gathered up the discus measuring tapes.

Step 1 – We noticed the bleachers appeared to be centered on both sides of the stadium, so we tied a string from the middle of the metal support located on the home bleachers to the corresponding metal support of the visitor's bleachers. The string became the 50-yard line.

Step 2 – The track had notches in the middle of the north and south curves. We tied a string from one end to the other and that gave us an intersection in the middle of the field.

Step 3 – To find the sidelines we knew we had to measure 80 feet from the middle of the field in both directions.

Step 4 – To establish where the back of the end zones would be, we measured 180 feet or 60 yards, each direction, from the mid-point.

Step 5 – Now that we had our mid-point, sidelines and back of our end zones we had to designate the corners. We did what all good coaches would do, we eyeballed it.

Culture Defeats Strategy 2 - Goonville, Texas Pop. 11

We checked and double-checked to make sure we were ok and determined our corners were fine. After four hours, we had the outline of a field.

Step 6 - The goal post installation instructions showed that the goal post base must be installed four feet behind the back line of the end zone. We spray painted an X at this location. Finally, we knew the exact location to install the goal posts.

Step 7 - Lastly, the installation instructions showed that the hole in the ground should be six feet deep and three feet in diameter! We were not fired up about digging that hole! Mr. Simpson was so impressed with our 'string' field, he decided to let the maintenance department finish the installation.'

CHAPTER 7 REVIEW
THE ELITE COACHING STAFF

- ☐ Elite coaches have a growth mindset.

- ☐ In today's world of easy access to knowledge there is no excuse to not grow every day. Books, podcasts, YouTube and Ted Talks are all out there for us to utilize.

- ☐ Sweat 30-minutes a day for maximum performance.

- ☐ There's a lot more to coaching than coaching. The easiest part of your day is putting on your whistle.

- ☐ Be a chief of staff for your POTUS. Loyalty, blue collar and being a tremendous observer is all a part of the elite assistant coach.

- ☐ Sometimes conflict has to occur. Chart and measure 'effort plays' and hold them accountable!

- ☐ Have your own core values as a coach. Take the time to think about the three core values you live by and write them down.

- ☐ The answer should always be YES.

CHAPTER 8

LESSON #7 - GOONVILLE IS BORN

> *"Yes sir! There are so many goons here it's like we are in Goonville."*
>
> John Taylor
> Offensive Lineman
> Senior 2019 - Original Goon

'We have a strong instinct to belong to small groups defined by a clear purpose and understanding,' author Sebastian Junger says to describe his book, 'Tribe.' People want to be part of a tribe. Grown men who weren't good on their high school team will wear an NFL jersey of their favorite player so they can feel more like they are on the team or a part of the group.

In the same way, every player wants to feel like the team he or she is on is special. Every team and every team member needs an identity. When we started instilling a much more intentional work ethic and discipline I knew we needed to give them some type of descriptive, personal term for an identity. We needed to find something to allow them to feel good about being on our team so I started calling them 'goons.' At first, this was totally private for us. Goon was a way for me to teach them our '1% better each day' mentality. I

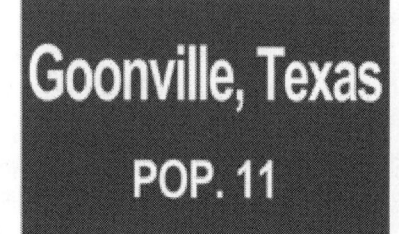

Culture Defeats Strategy 2 - Goonville, Texas Pop. 11

told them, "Goons do not care about the weather, they don't care about the scoreboard, the officials, and certainly not our competition." I could tell they were latching on to it when I would say something like, "A goon is comfortable being uncomfortable. A goon will attack these 200's and not care."

There is no telling how many times I have been asked how we came up with the term 'Goonville.' About six weeks after my arrival at NF was the district track meet. I was walking around during the field events when I came up on the triple jump. NF was responsible for running off this event so we had a few coaches and players working. Some of our offensive linemen were raking the sand between jumps when I walked up and said, "I'm a proud coach seeing all you goons working and raking the pit." "Yes sir! There are so many goons here it's like we're in Goonville," said sophomore John Taylor.

Oh my, I knew immediately this was something I could work with and capitalize on. My mind started processing how I could take Goonville and make it a 'place.' Goonville, Texas, Population 11 would make an outstanding city limit sign to post at the entrance of our locker room.

GOON
Grit
Obsessed
One %
better

During this time, we were having our guys earn their way into the 'Elite locker room.' After the track meet and the phrase Goonville was born, and for each one who qualified I would take his pic and tweet out,

'Another resident of Goonville, Texas.' Boom! The players and parents loved it. We were on to something

@CoachJacksonTPW   #culturematters

Culture Defeats Strategy 2 - Goonville, Texas Pop. 11

that would generate some energy that the north side of Forney badly needed.

I know the word can have a negative meaning so we were very deliberate about making it personal for us. After the 2017 season we took it a step farther and defined it as 'grit - obsessed - one percent better each day - next play'.

WORDS HAVE POWER

There is power in words. The military uses the term 'casualties' over deaths because soldiers are not as affected by it. Businesses will say 'sign some paperwork' instead of 'sign a contract' because we aren't as intimidated by this verbiage. An example that makes sense to me is to compare these three similar words; enthusiasm, energy, and juice. Every player on your team will be more fascinated or prefer juice over energy or enthusiasm.

WORDS ARE YOUR BRAND

In an iconic scene from the movie, 'The Founder,' Dick McDonald and Ray Kroc have a conversation on the day Kroc officially purchased the rights to the name 'McDonalds,' one of the brothers, Dick McDonald, asked Kroc,

"That day we met and showed you the tour. We showed you everything. The whole system, all our secrets, we were an open book. So why didn't you just..."

Culture Defeats Strategy 2 - Goonville, Texas Pop. 11

"Steal it? Grab your ideas and just start my own company? It would have failed," said Kroc.

"Why is that?" asked McDonald.

"Am I the only one who got the kitchen tour? You must have invited lots of people back there. How many of them succeeded?" Kroc asks. "Lots of people started restaurants," McDonald says. "As big as McDonalds? No one ever has and no one ever will because they all lacked one thing that makes McDonalds special," Kroc explains.

"Which is," McDonald asks.

"Even *you* don't know what it is? It's not just the system Dick, it's the name. That glorious name, *McDonalds*. It can be anything you want it to be. It's limitless. It's wide open, it sounds like.... America. A guy named McDonald, he's never going to get pushed around in life. I knew the first time I saw that name on your stand out there I had to have it."

Kroc understood the power of a name. The power of words and an identity. He says later in the scene, "Do you think people would buy a burger from a place called Kroc's?" I knew the Falcons needed an identity. All programs who are down either need a new one or life pumped into one from years ago.

Culture Defeats Strategy 2 - Goonville, Texas Pop. 11

> **"Words create worlds."**
> Pierre du Plessis
>
> **"Words have the power to make things happen."**
> Frederick Buechner

YOUR CULTURE IS YOUR BRAND

Your brand is the consistent image that pops into people's heads when they think about your program. It is the image that is bigger than success and loss on the field, it is standing for something no one else stands for.

Matt Rhule spoke about the brand of the Baylor Bear football team and compared it to Pepsi. "When you open a can of Pepsi you know what you're getting. If there were a million cans in front of you it wouldn't matter which one you chose. Each of them would taste the same. We want our players to be this way; all of them playing the game the same way. Our brand at Baylor is that we are striving to be the toughest, hardest-working and most competitive team in the country. When you play the Bears, you'll get this! We make our team say this over and over again."

You must analyze where the players are mentally when you take over a new program. Each situation is different so you must handle each one accordingly. In 2010, at Poteet, they needed to feel good about being on the football team. Job #1 was to instill confidence. When I arrived at Grapevine in 2014 I felt like we lacked toughness. It took a while but we became a blue-collar, genuinely tough team in an area with lots of Starbucks and white-collar families. The players at NF were hungry, but lacked discipline and there was lot of selfish behavior. I went with the 'it's my way or the highway' message while still making sure they knew I was rooting for them to make it.

We talked often to our team about Goonville and how they would always be remembered as 'original goons.'

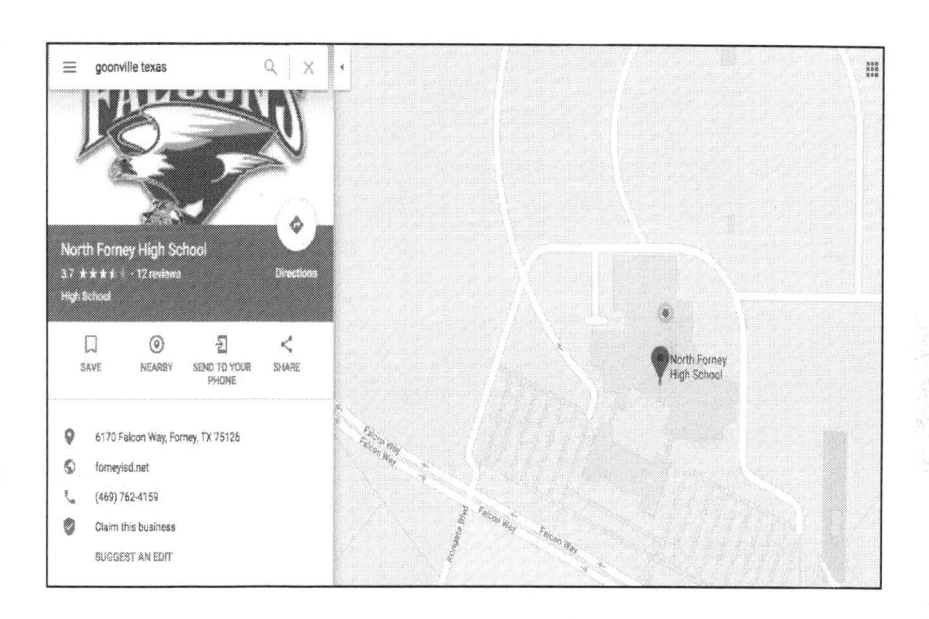

[Screenshot of Google Maps search for "goonville texas" showing North Forney High School, 6170 Falcon Way, Forney, TX 75126, forneyisd.net, (469) 762-4159]

This was important to them. They will be a part of the group who invented the tribe. If they could make big personal changes to help the team win more games the more they would be remembered and leave a legacy.

> **"We want tempo to be a lifestyle, how you live your life. The decisions you make affect so many people. It's a brand. That's the biggest thing we want our guys to understand. This is far more than just a saying."**
>
> **Chad Morris**

SEASON REVIEW

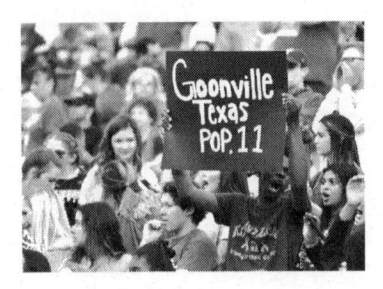

For much of this book I have described how tough things were and how much change our guys had to be willing to make for it to be a TPW type culture. In this chapter, we are going to get into the good stuff. Most of you are not reading this because you want to relive the 2017 North Forney football season. But, the lessons are in the struggle. This will be the fun stuff of how a program, school and even a community became Goonville, Texas, Population 11.

Let's recap our season a little at a time. We finished our non-district schedule 3-0 and won our first district game at home 70-65. No, that's not a misprint. We defeated Wylie East by five points in a game that took years off my life. Colby Suits, our quarterback, accounted for 10 touchdowns in the win! This was the most touchdowns scored in Texas in over 50 years by one player! Colby had 193 yards with four touchdowns rushing and 407 yards and six touchdowns passing.

Next, we lost to eventual state champion Highland Park 63-42 at Highlander Stadium, where they had won 105 of the last 106 games. We were down 49-42 in the fourth quarter but never could get a turnover or big mistake by the Scots (one reason they are so good).

We were 1-1 in district and had to travel to Poteet for their homecoming that I wrote about earlier. This is one of the wins every turnaround team has to have. A legitimate upset and confidence-booster.

The following week we played Royse City at home. In one of our best overall performances of the year we knocked off the Bulldogs, 67-28.

We were feeling good about our 6-1 overall record and more importantly, our 3-1 league mark. Offensively, we were scoring 57 points per game, getting better on defense and our culture was starting to take hold. During the first six games of the year we had at least one player suspended for four of them. This is worth repeating; I haven't had to suspend that

many players in my 17-year head coaching career combined before 2017. It was tough to deal with the issues but the message was finally getting received. We were getting better each week, the vibe at the school was terrific and the community was on fire. We could have sold anything with "Goonville" printed on it.

A BITTER DEFEAT THAT TESTED OUR CULTURE

Our next opponent, the Lovejoy Leopards, had only won two games the entire season. What could go wrong?

Lovejoy has been a solid program for several years. Coach Todd Ford and his staff always do a great job, but they had struggled this season. They started 0-5, but had won the last two. I knew they would be a challenge. They were getting healthy and the game was on the road. To make matters worse for our players' mindset, one of their losses was to Highland Park, 50-7. HP was the squad we had played with for most of the game.

We have a weekly 48-hour countdown meeting, an idea I stole from the late Don James, head coach of the Washington Huskies. He believed 24 hours was not long enough to start the mental clock before a game.

I was concerned we were playing the 2-0 Leopards and not the 0-5 ones. I decided to go with the theme of the 'horse racing form' for our meeting. I have been to a horse track maybe twice in the last 20 years so I don't know a lot about horse racing in general or the intricate racing form. For a guy like me, the form has a lot of confusing numbers and stats. Most of the data deals with past performances with the last two or three races being the most relevant. I took an example of a form, enlarged it and used it to warn our guys about not looking at the Leopards' 2-5 overall record. "If Lovejoy were a race horse there would be some smart money on them. They would go off at favorable odds because they haven't won many races but the last two would show the experienced handicapper they have gotten healthy and are a different horse now."

Bill Belichick also used a horse race as an example with the Patriots a few years ago. He showed them a clip of a race with five or six horses near the front as they entered the back stretch. He paused the video and asked, "We have watched most of this race. Which horse is going to win? He let it run a few

Culture Defeats Strategy 2 - Goonville, Texas Pop. 11

more seconds and asked them again, "There are several horses close to the front. Can any of you tell for sure which one is going to pull away for the victory? No, you can't, just like no one can predict who is going to win the AFC East with four games remaining." He did not show them the end of the race.

Things did not go our way during the night we played at Lovejoy. They wanted it more than we did. We got out-coached and out-played. The final score was 43-41 but it felt much worse. We played without emotion or any sense of urgency. We acted like a team that had 'arrived' and it was embarrassing.

After the game, one of our coaches said, "When we get back to the fieldhouse we need to address some negativity after the game. A few of our guys are complaining in the locker room."

There isn't much I can wait on in general. An attitude issue ranks way up there on my list of impatience so I got up as fast as I could and went into the locker room. "Somebody in here not happy with how others played tonight?!? I am being very loud. I was tired, frustrated and bitterly disappointed about not only the loss but how we played. The news of complaining hit me like a sledgehammer on my heart. "Is that what I'm hearing? Is there anyone in here who wants to complain about something? We just got our butts kicked so I guess we are going back to our old attitudes? Are you three (some of our better seniors and leaders) in here complaining about your teammates and coaches?!?

One of the players was wearing headphones and didn't take them off as I was addressing them. When I asked him to take them off he gave an attitude I wasn't ready

Culture Defeats Strategy 2 - Goonville, Texas Pop. 11

for. He said, "the music isn't on so I don't need to take them off." Oh my. That was tough to hear after we had come so far.

I'm not sure I handled it right. These are the situations that make coaching so hard. Every situation is different and it takes experience to maneuver through them. I was not doing much in this situation except going bull in a china shop. You get what you tolerate, so if I am going to err it is going to be in not tolerating selfishness or finger-pointing. This is why you must put them in pressure situations during offseason and practice. A culture must survive adversity. Ours wasn't holding up under the strain of a disappointing loss.

After we got back to the high school we had all three players come into the coaches' office. I wanted to address it with them as a group now that everyone was calm, especially me. We talked through it and while none of us felt great afterwards I sure felt better by not waiting and going to sleep that night with it heavy on my mind.

The next morning, the mom of the player who originally refused to take off his headphones, asked if she and her son could meet with me. She wanted to know exactly what happened and if her son being disrespectful, which I totally respect. I decided to have the meeting with the entire staff. This was going to be a watershed week for this team so we had better circle of the wagons as a staff starting right then.

We went through the entire situation with her. The locker room after the game, where I told her I may have overreacted, to the comment about the headphones and not getting a real sense of contrition in the coaches' office once we got back to NF. The mom and I both did our best to get the point across it wasn't going to be a big deal until the headphones became an issue. This is a player we had not had any issues with so this was a teachable moment I felt like was getting through to him.

When they left, I thanked her for coming and helping us get some closure with the situation. She responded with, "**thank you, coaches. This is more than football, we are raising men here.**" Amen.

> *"Failure is simply the opportunity to begin again, this time more intelligently."*
> **Henry Ford**
>
> *"Try again. Fail again. Fail better."*
> **Samuel Beckett**

WHAT WE NEEDED

The loss affected me more than it should have. I couldn't shake it for most of the week. An elite leader says much more neutral and focuses on how deliberate practice can make his/her team better.

It was exactly what we needed. It refocused us and made us realize we had not arrived yet. It was like someone had displayed the 'Mission Accomplished' sign on the aircraft carrier. One of the dangers of a team enjoying success for the first time is they can enjoy it too much and lose the 'crumb-eater' mentality they had.

Culture Defeats Strategy 2 - Goonville, Texas Pop. 11

Week 9 was basically a must-win game at home to another team NF had not beaten before, the West Mesquite Wranglers. With our loss to Lovejoy we were in a bind at 3-2 in district play, but West also needed a win to guarantee themselves a berth in the postseason.

Sr. receiver Corey Mayfield makes a huge fourth down reception vs. West Mesquite.

The Wranglers were loaded with several Division 1 college prospects. They are an established program that would be tough to beat, to say the least. I kept this to myself, but it was a terrible feeling to think about the possibility of us not getting in the playoffs if we couldn't pull this one out. We had come so far it would have been a tough pill to swallow.

We got off to a great start as Corey Mayfield ran back the opening kickoff 97 yards for a touchdown. This was just what we needed, but after holding them on their first possession they 'scooped and scored' a fumble by us to tie the game at 7-7. We went back and forth with them for most of the game. Our tempo (we snapped the ball 95 times in the game) and running back Calvin Ribera - along with

Sr. quarterback Colby Suits and I after he scores vs. West Mesquite.

our tremendous offensive line - put the game away in the fourth quarter. Another key stat for us was we were 14-20 on third down conversions. The tired Wranglers continued to play hard but we made first down after first down late to come away with a much-needed 50-44 victory.

A week earlier our culture was shaky, but we had a great week of practice and with this win everything was back where we had been. We were refocused and ready to move closer as a team. We had our 'mojo' back. There is good and bad in everything, even a loss.

THE UNITY BOWL VS. FORNEY

We were 7-2 entering our final regular season game, the Unity Bowl. We had already qualified for the playoffs, and had beaten Poteet and West Mesquite for the first time in school history. We had another monkey to get off our back and that was to beat our cross-town rival for the first time also.

Forney had dominated the series going back to the first time they met in 2012. The Jackrabbits had won by an avg. of 23 points so this was not as much of a true rivalry as a 'big brother' vs. 'little brother' matchup.

Beating Poteet was great for me personally, having coached there from 2010-2012, and West Mesquite was also very satisfying because we had never beaten them in my three seasons at Poteet. Forney was big for our guys, the school and our community. As coaches, we could feel the weight of the streak had on everyone.

Culture Defeats Strategy 2 - Goonville, Texas Pop. 11

North Forney was the little brother that needed to feel like it was all grown up.

We never talked about the game or the Jackrabbits during the year. For us, it is always 'win today.' We love to say, 'nameless, faceless opponent,' we worry about us and if we play our game the result will take care of itself. This game was different though. Just like we had to see if we could rebound after the Lovejoy loss, the Unity Bowl would show if we could handle success again after qualifying for the playoffs. This would be a test to see if we were ready to win playoff games or would we lose our discipline and do dumb stuff on social media or in the community.

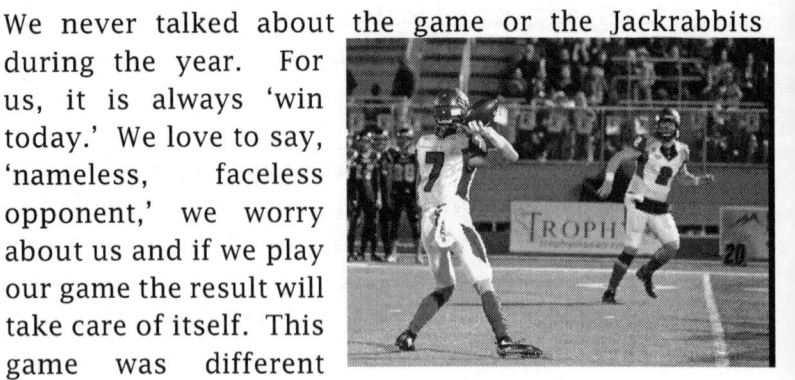

Sr. receiver Jordan Carroll completing a 'throwback to the quarterback' to Colby Suits vs. Forney

Forney is a great town with a population of approximately 15,000, located 25 miles east of Dallas. Forney High School and North Forney are separated by State Highway 80. South is 'old Forney' with a neat downtown area. There are businesses that have been around for decades. North of the highway is where most of the new growth is occurring. There are several housing editions that have sprung up in the last decade with lots of move-ins from Dallas County and the surrounding areas.

@CoachJacksonTPW   #culturematters

Culture Defeats Strategy 2 - Goonville, Texas Pop. 11

Forney has a great tradition in many sports, especially in football. Understandably, the Falcons have struggled through the years versus the established Jackrabbit program. It was time to turn the tide in 2017. We had the talent and it was late enough in the season where we were firing on all cylinders.

Both schools share City Bank Stadium, which is located on the campus of Forney High School. City Bank has a capacity of 9,000 and it was an electric venue on this night. We were the visiting team wearing all white uniforms. Our crowd came through for us. They brought the juice by being loud and waving white and blue 'Goon' towels as we kicked off.

Principal Courtney Sharkey and I with the 'Unity Bowl' trophy

Our team did a great job of staying in the moment and not allowing a game to be too big for them. We were focused and played well from the get-go. In the first quarter, **Corey Mayfield** caught a 41-yard touchdown pass from Colby Suits and Jayden Barrall followed it with a 21-yard reception for a touchdown later in the first quarter. As we expected, Forney was playing inspired early and we were in dogfight. Sophomore Glen De La Hoz made one of the biggest plays of the game when he intercepted a pass in the end zone to stop a deep possession by the Jackrabbits.

@CoachJacksonTPW   #culturematters

Culture Defeats Strategy 2 - Goonville, Texas Pop. 11

Our offense erupted in the second quarter with four straight scores in a span of five minutes. Suits scored a 1-yard rushing touchdown, then caught a 14-yard touchdown pass from Jordan Carroll on a fly sweep pass back to the QB. Suits and Carroll connected twice more with 39-yard and 35-yard touchdowns. We scored 27 points to essentially put the game away at the half with a score of 42-12.

Like most coaches, I have been on both sidelines in a blowout rivalry game. We ran the ball and finished the contest as quickly as possible in the second half. We needed to stay healthy entering the 5A playoffs for the first time in school history and there was no need to rub salt in the wound of a good man, Kevin Rush, the head coach of the Jackrabbits. When the final horn sounded we had closed out the regular season with a 49-19 victory and an 8-2 overall record. It had been nine months since we had arrived but they were now trusting our system and process. It is satisfying and fun to write this. It feels good to think back to all the struggles we had early in the season and to reminisce about how we had changed as a program as we entered the playoffs. If we had not had a group of young men who let go of their old ways and gotten in the 'Goonville wheelbarrow' so to speak, our season would have ended after 10 games.

As good as things were, we still didn't have a gold ball to put in the trophy case. We would have to win a playoff game to make that happen.

PLAYOFFS - ROUND 1 vs PINE TREE

In Texas, four teams from each district make the playoffs and all games leading up to the state championship are at neutral sites. One of the toughest things to do is find a place suitable and agreeable to both teams for the first round (bi-district) game. With so many games taking place that first weekend it is a scramble to say the least.

Pine Tree High School is located in Longview, Texas. There are not a lot of stadiums large enough to host a 5A playoff game between our two towns so this made it even tougher. Another factor is trying to stay in your routine of playing on Friday night which is what most coaches want to do. We got lucky and found newly-renovated Bruce Field in Athens.

Athens High School is a classification smaller than us (4A) so the stadium was not huge. When Pine Tree head coach Kerry Lane and I met there the Saturday before to look at the stadium and discuss officials, who would be the home team, etc. it was immediately obvious the visiting stands would not hold an excited North Forney community. Another interesting quirk about playoff games in Texas is how many things are decided on a coin flip. Which team will be designated the home team is one of the first things to be decided and we needed to win the flip or I would have issues with a fan base not having enough room. The quarter bounced our way and we were the home team...whew.

We were the better team on paper. These seniors had accomplished a lot of 'firsts' but we could sense they were not satisfied. We had a good week of practice with no drama, which was becoming the norm now (hallelujah).

I love routines and systems. More importantly, teams must have them so they are not having to think about things other than the task on hand.

Our 'goons' seemed very focused in pre-game warmups. We came out with a swinging gate trick play on the first play of scrimmage that went for 69 yards and scored soon after on a Colby Suits quarterback run.

We hit on another 'special' as we call them (gadget type play) when receiver Jackson Ennels connected with Corey Mayfield for a 48-yard touchdown on a double pass play.

ROUND 2 vs. LAKE DALLAS at AT&T STADIUM

Usually, the Texas state football championships are held at AT&T Stadium, the home of the Dallas Cowboys. For a lucky few, some schools are also allowed to use it for playoff games when it is available.

I have coached at AT&T before and it is a test of discipline in many ways. Teams can get enamored by all the 'bells and whistles' and not focus on the task at hand. In the middle of the stadium hanging from the roof is the biggest replay board in the world. It stretches from 30-yard line to 30-yard line. I always tell my team they are not allowed to look at this board during the game. I know this sounds odd but you must do all you can to keep the game what it is, a game and not a fantasy football experience.

Culture Defeats Strategy 2 - Goonville, Texas Pop. 11

Amazingly, a team that struggled for so long to not drive me crazy with their undisciplined behavior was now as focused and 'on point' as any team I had ever coached. Once again, they did not seem to worry about any of the externals. They stayed in the present and were very business-like during our week of practice. One of our wide receiver coaches, Justin Velasquez, was a member of our 2010 Poteet team that had gone from 1-19 to 12-3 his senior year. One of the biggest wins we had was a 45-28 defeat of 12-0 Highland Park at AT&T. "This team reminds me of our 2010 team, coach. They are on a mission just like we were," he would tell me occasionally, and I would agree with him every time.

Willie Thomas with one of his two interceptions vs. Lake Dallas

This was Thanksgiving week so it was another challenge. We were out of our normal routine. We even had a 'Goonsgiving' practice on Thanksgiving morning and invited the public to attend. Our booster club had coffee, hot chocolate, donuts and of course, Goonville merchandise for sell. We had a lot a great crowd settle in our indoor facility to watch our guys go through a 70-minute practice.

Saturday finally arrived. We were the middle game of a tripleheader with a 4:00 p.m. kickoff. One of the challenges of this situation is each team only has 45-minutes to warm up. This is a pretty big change in our normal routine of going out 60 minutes before game

Culture Defeats Strategy 2 - Goonville, Texas Pop. 11

time. We had walked through this the day before and put them there mentally to understand everything would happen faster. Instead of having 25 minutes between warmup and kickoff it would be 15 minutes.

They handled warmups like a champ. They were locked in just like the week before in Athens. I am still so impressed how this group did not get 'big-eyed' by anything during the playoffs.

We won the toss and kept our trend of taking the ball and starting the game out with an unusual formation. We started out in what we call 'ninja,' four offensive linemen split wide to the left with two receivers with them. We had a receiver split wide right and only our center, tight end, quarterback and running back near the ball. One reason I did this was to show our guys the second round at AT&T wasn't a big deal. We were not scared to show 20,000 people how we play. On the fourth play of the drive Colby Suits threw a slant to Jordan Carroll for a 25-yard touchdown. After Carlos Rodriguez converted the extra point we were up 7-0 with less than a minute off the clock.

Sr. tight end Michael Court with a 72-yard reception at AT&T Stadium

We played a complete game that left no doubt we would be a tough out in the playoffs. The score at half was 30-0 and we never looked back. The final was 50-20 and we had shown a lot of people North Forney was for real.

@CoachJacksonTPW   #culturematters

Willie Thomas, a senior linebacker and one of our leaders, had a great game. He had two big interceptions and 11 tackles.

ROUND 3 vs. MANSFIELD LEGACY

Our next opponent would be the best team we would see all season. Mansfield Legacy had more talent than either West Mesquite or Mesquite Poteet. They were a complete team led by head coach Chris Melson.

The game was played at Eagle Stadium, the home of the Allen Eagles. It is known nationwide as the 60-million-dollar venue (one of the most expensive in the country) for only one high school team.

We stayed in our new Saturday routine and played a rare day game. Mansfield Legacy was all we anticipated. The game was a physical war. We ran 103 plays and wore them down in the second half but could not overcome our slow start. They were the better team but we had our chances. I could not have been prouder of our effort as we fell 45-35.

After the game, our fans acted different than any group I have ever seen. They cheered and thanked everyone. Instead of blaming the coaches (happens A LOT after a playoff loss) they were truly grateful for the season. I will never forget walking by our side of the stadium and numerous parents standing at the rail telling every player and coach who walked by 'thank you' and 'we are proud of you.' It was amazing. The change had happened. An entire program and community had bought in to our core values and our Goonville, Texas culture.

YOU'RE CRAZY IF YOU THINK OLD WAYS WILL FIX A PROBLEM

The great preacher Tony Evans tells this story about getting 'to the root of the problem.' In the early part of the 1900's, there was a crude test to see if a mental patient was sane enough to be released back into society. The patient was placed in a room with a sink. The faucet was turned on and a stopper was put in the drain until the sink overflowed. The patient was then handed a mop and the door was closed. If the patient had enough sense to shut off the water, pull the plug, and then mop up the water, he or she was considered capable of going home. But on the other hand, if the patient mopped like crazy and never bothered to shut off the water and/or pull the plug, he or she was considered still insane and needed to be detained for a longer period in the mental institution.

As I have stated earlier, I love stories because they create mental pictures in our brains. This story relates to the topic of the daily 'fist-fight.' Throughout this book I have painted the picture of where we were and what we did to change it. If you don't attack it daily with an intentional plan of core values and team meetings you are just mopping and letting the water run. A great culture only happens when we turn off the faucet.

Several stories about how we were growing our culture were tough for me to relive again. This chapter of telling our story of changed attitudes was definitely the most fun of any of the chapters. Some of the things we did were pretty harsh. I knew for us to turn off the faucet we had to have zero tolerance for anything below our standard, yet still find a way to love them into a true team.

It was my honor to write this book. Brian Cain, Peak Performance expert, told me before I wrote the original Culture Defeats Strategy in 2016 that all non-fiction books must solve a problem. The author will not have an audience to help if he or she is not helping people improve in some way. This made a lot of sense to me. I have tried hard to make sure neither book was about much about me or my teams. My goal was to help leaders through some of my experiences.

UNCONVENTIONAL

In 1967, the #1 band in the U.S. was The Monkees. Yes, The Monkees were more popular than The Beatles and The Rolling Stones combined. The 'teenybopper' sensations had four #1 albums in 1967 alone and a very popular television show.

Culture Defeats Strategy 2 - Goonville, Texas Pop. 11

In the summer of that year, at the height of their popularity, the Monkees booked a 28-city tour across America and England. They hired an unknown musician to be the opening act. He was very different from the Monkees, in fact, he was different from just about any musician ever.

The Monkees selected Jimi Hendrix to be their opening act for the tour. In the middle of his set on the first night of performances, the crowd began to boo. It progressively got louder but he finished his set. The next night it happened again. Word began to spread that The Monkees had a terrible opening act. Each night the audience, made up of teenage, Caucasian girls, booed Hendrix. The displeasure of the mob was expressed more quickly at each venue. Finally, on July 17, the eighth date on the tour, as Jimi Hendrix walked onto the stage, he was met with thousands of fans yelling, 'boo,' 'get off the stage,' 'boo!!' That was it. Hendrix had had enough so he saluted the crowd with his middle finger and walked away from his big break with The Monkees.

Jimi Hendrix was unconventional and ahead of his time. He had the guts to stay true to himself. He could have easily changed for the audiences so he could have kept making big money and more importantly big exposure. I told my then 17-year old son, Russ this story and he had no idea who The Monkees were. He knew exactly who Jimi Hendrix was.

I normally start most of my Culture Factory

presentations with this story of one of the oddest pairings of musical groups of all time, but it is a great one to end this book with. Jimi Hendrix was unconventional. If he would have changed to be popular to the Monkees crowd, Russ probably wouldn't know him either. For your program to be remembered, think unconventionally. The most common coaches out there are good at scheme and strength, speed and agility training. An unconventional culture is the edge.

Benjamin Franklin said that we all need to either live a life worth writing about or write something worth reading. The story of the 2017 North Forney Falcons was worth telling. How a few adults changed the culture and how a bunch of players put their egos aside and 'got in the wheelbarrow' is worth writing about. I don't care where your program or organization is now, if you are willing to be deliberate in creating a championship culture and tough enough to get in the 'daily fist-fight' you will change it. If this book helped you a little in doing so I am truly blessed.

Go change a culture. Your people deserve to be in a great one

Before you read this chapter from Steven Carroll I want to say THANK YOU to Steven and all the booster club members who were ready to serve when I began at North Forney.

From the beginning, all they wanted to know was 'what can we do for you, coach to help make this what you want?' It was such a blessing to be surrounded by a group of adults who did not have any agenda other than serving the kids and the new coaching staff.

Culture Defeats Strategy 2 - Goonville, Texas Pop. 11

Glen DeLaHoz and John Tracy, the following booster club presidents, THANK YOU as well! North Forney is a special place. It is the rare place where parents want us to help raise their children and we are 'celebrated not tolerated'.

I am so blessed and thank God for allowing me to be the head coach of the North Forney Falcons!

CHAPTER 9

'THE ANSWER IS YES' by Steven Carroll - Booster Club President

I will never forget the 2017 Football Season in Goonville, TX (North Forney). The transformation that took place in a matter of 10 months was nothing short of miraculous, and I believe, was one of the greatest "Divine Intervention" moments I have personally experienced. For me, It all began with a simple phrase, "The Answer is YES!"

Every parent wants to see their kids have incredible life experiences. My wife and I are no different. We want to see our kids succeed and have the opportunity to contribute to and be a part of something greater than themselves. We want their dreams to come true and have moments they will never forget. We desire to champion their personality, celebrate their accomplishments, and encourage them to love what they do and do what they love for the rest of their lives. We, like all parents, believe that our kids are the best thing that ever walked the planet, and at times it is hard to see those hopes and dreams come face to face with reality and disappointment. But as you know, it's not what happens to you in life that is most important, but how you deal with what happens to you.

As adults, parents, & coaches, we recognize that the journey to unforgettable moments isn't comfortable. It's difficult. Difficulties are necessary to shape us and our futures. We'd all rather have exciting, fun, and life-changing experiences without going through pain and struggle, but life doesn't work that way. That's why we want our kids\players to know...

"Life isn't easy."
"The struggle will truly make you stronger."
"Do the right thing."
"Trust the process."
"Believe there is a divine plan bigger than you."
"Submit to and trust leadership."
"Show up. Be on time. Give 110%."

We want quotes like these to serve as principles to help our children know how to adjust and respond during life-shaping moments. But, we can't teach something that we haven't been able to acknowledge and admit personally. How we react as an adult and the mentality with which we approach life, along with the players & families we lead, is, without a doubt, shaped by the culture we grow up in and that we surround ourselves with as we live out our lives. Culture matters!

Over the last 25 years, my wife and I have been blessed to have the opportunity to parent four children. We've had to choose to be aware of their giftings, personalities, and limitations. It's not easy. As parents, we by nature believe our kids are fantastic at everything, which is normal, but we must choose to be responsible enough to create a culture in our home that teaches them that nothing is given...everything is earned. Life doesn't just hand you what you want. That's why we, as parents, whether we realize it or not, need leaders like you in the lives of our kids. We need coaches, teachers, and mentors that will partner with us to take our kids to levels we can't.

I have adopted the philosophy in serving others, that the "Answer is YES!" It's not my job as a parent and former booster club president to shape the culture of a football program. It's was my job to support the coach and follow their lead. Every parent or booster club member doesn't think like I do (although I highly encourage you to find that person within your program that does), but I do believe you can foster that mentality within the culture you create. Then your parents and boosters will put confidence in you and not only support you 100% with their resources, but more importantly, they will entrust you with their children.

Parents and boosters are a powerful force! They can be a great benefit to your success as a coach. When leading in the right direction, as you create a culture in your program, they will get behind you, and everyone can have moments & experiences that no one will ever never forget.

When Coach Jackson showed up at North Forney High School, the culture that was in place was primarily negative. It was a culture of defeat, uncertainty, inconsistency, and a lack of overall leadership. Our team didn't have an identity. There were great athletes and an active parent base. We had been 'drifting in the wind' for several years, but there was a definite lack of trust and belief. The result? A constant state of

Culture Defeats Strategy 2 - Goonville, Texas Pop. 11

dissension, mistrust, and negativity. The program was filled with parents that thought, and even believed, they could do it better. The conversations around every dinner table and among all the dads was that there needed to be a change. As you can imagine, there's nothing positive about that.

In the fall of 2014, 2 1/2 years before Coach Jackson arrived, our son was entering the football program at North Forney as a freshman. We were all so excited about Texas High School Football & Friday Night Lights, but there was also a general sense of reservation & doubt about the football program. The team's record was 6-24 under the leadership that was in place, and several families had great athletes, that chose to move and put their sons in other schools with better football programs.

Even with those families leaving, we knew there were still very talented players on the team and others coming into the program, many of which had played and won together since they were little, and so at least that was something we could grab hold of. We chose as a family to engage and try to make a difference in whatever way we could. So, with that mindset, I attended my first football booster club meeting in August of 2014.

There were five people at the booster club meeting that evening. I was shocked that more parents weren't there and were very surprised that there was only one dad. All the officers were moms, and it is evident that these ladies were not only working very hard, and doing all they could but didn't get much support from other families within the program. No one was excited about the NF football. No one expected to win. No one seemed

@CoachJacksonTPW   #culturematters

to really care. There was a group of Dad's that set up the run through the tunnel each week, but every one of them was frustrated, disenchanted, and disappointed. They knew there was a lack of culture, leadership, and direction within the program, and they felt helpless after years of struggle.

I had committed to getting involved to see where I could plug in and help. After attending the booster meeting, I met the existing head coach, who was a great guy, that inherited a challenging situation and set of circumstances. He was headed into his 3rd season at NF, but there didn't seem to be a light at the end of the tunnel. He asked if I would become the Team Chaplain, and I was more than happy to help (Remember, the answer is "Yes"). During that first season on the sidelines as the chaplain, I watched the varsity go 1-9. The lack of a real, tangible culture was glaringly evident as the seniors and parents were obviously very frustrated and disappointed. The parents that had been leading the booster club were obviously ready to move on, so at the conclusion of the 2014 season I became the booster club president. The first objective was to get more dad's involved, so I called a buddy of mine who became VP & another dad agreed to become the treasurer. With the help of some other awesome moms and dads, we began

to build a foundation of folks that were ready and willing to say
"Yes!"

Over the next two seasons, this team of booster club leaders began to add more board positions and build momentum & support. I continued serving as team chaplain. As chaplain, we started a game day Breakfast of Champions & prayer before the games. I made sure there was breakfast each week, and we enlisted inspirational and motivational speakers before every game. One week I was even able to secure LSU Legend and former Dallas Cowboy defensive lineman Marcus Spears. The boosters & families at North Forney provided meals, made cool game day shirts to sell, helped get the gear the coach needed, and were willing to do all we could to make the program better, but we also learned a valuable lesson. Creating a culture is not the chaplain, parents, community, or boosters' responsibility. All of the "great stuff" we were doing was needed and is a vital part of any great program, but those things should provide support and enhance whatever culture the head coach and his staff create.

In 2015 the majority of starters on the varsity team were sophomores within my son's class, except for a couple of positive senior leaders. It was like a relaunching of sorts, but the young squat went 2-8, and a negative culture still seemed to dominate the fiber of the squad. There was a renewed sense of excitement as the 2016 season approached. The team was a year older; they had a pretty good offseason, many of the players were getting outside work and wanted to improve, the booster club change was in full effect, more support and positivity was surrounding the program. Even with all that happening, our team still went 4-6.

Everyone was so disappointed, the players most of all. We all wanted it so bad! Again, the one thing that was clearer than ever before was that no matter how many "good" things we all did to support the team, we couldn't change the culture or cast vision for the program. That had to be done from the top down. Yes, there was a foundation of support forming, and we were all ready to say "Yes," but we needed someone to show us the way. That's when Coach Randy Jackson entered the picture in February of 2017. The moment he arrived on campus, the culture began to change immediately, everything began to matter, and Goonville, TX, was born!

They say hindsight is 20/20, and that has never been truer than as I type these words. As I look back on the transformation that happened at North Forney since 2017, there is no way I can adequately put into words the many moments, experiences, and joy those ten months brought to all of us. We will all be marked for the rest of our lives by what happened that season. Why? Because the culture finally changed. The direction was in place. We had a leader who brought in other leaders that knew what it would take to point the program in the right direction.

The cultural shift began to happen before Coach Jackson was ever officially hired. The moment he walked into the room as a candidate for the head coach, those of us from the North Forney community on the panel knew it was apparent he was the man for the job. What caused him to stand out? The statement and philosophy that "Culture over Strategy" matters most. When we heard him say "great strategy is only part of what wins games, you have to change the culture before a team can be successful," We not only knew that is what

Culture Defeats Strategy 2 - Goonville, Texas Pop. 11

we needed most, but that Coach Jackson wasn't just talking about it, he had done it!

His first official moment on campus as our head coach was at our annual football banquet. He got up and said only a few words, but they were powerful. I can't remember everything that he said, but these are the words that mattered to me, "I'm excited to be here at North Forney. We're going to change the culture, and we're going to win."

After the banquet was over, we immediately had a booster club officers meeting with Coach Jackson. It was apparent from the first moment he walked into the room that real change was coming, and we were ready. The first thing he did was pass out an agenda for the next ten months. It had everything on it! It was beautiful! Crazy how a simple schedule can feel like you are holding gold in your hands. That's what direction feels like to the people that want you to lead them. It's valuable!

The agenda included dates for:
- Parent information meeting to cast vision & set direction.
- Boot camp
- Spring football daily practice schedule culminating with a spring game.
- Summer workout schedule
- MOM's 101
- Polish and Pray (moms program night before games)
- Breakfast of Champions
- Scrimmage game date
- First game
- Homecoming

Culture Defeats Strategy 2 - Goonville, Texas Pop. 11

- Senior Night
- First playoff game
- Thanksgiving Day practice
- Heck, he even had us in the State Championship Game!

As I held that simple piece of paper in my hand, hope and excitement filled my soul. We had a vision. We had direction. I read every detail of that agenda, and for a moment, everyone else in the room seemed to disappear, and I said out loud, "coach, this piece of paper is like water to a group of people that have been in the desert for three years."

The rest, as they say, is Goonville, TX History. Coach Jackson hit every date on that agenda, and we all went to work. He surrounded himself with coaches that would implement his vision and believe in the culture. Booster club meetings grew in attendance and became exciting. We had our bumps in the road at times, but the answer was always "Yes." Coach Jackson would tell us what was needed, and our incredible team of leaders and parents would make it happen.

I remember the first booster club meeting after he was on campus. He made a list of what he'd like to get initially on the whiteboard. In fact, I have a picture of it saved on my phone. The file was comprised of a drone (we have three now), TV's (for both locker rooms, the hall, and the weight room), sound system, injury tent, conference table, and headphones. Within a matter of weeks, we got it all, and that was just the beginning. We bought new helmets, work out gear, uniforms, and whatever was needed to help support and develop the new culture Coach Jackson was building.

@CoachJacksonTPW #culturematters

Culture Defeats Strategy 2 – Goonville, Texas Pop. 11

My son, his fellow seniors, and the rest of the team, for the most part, bought into the culture, Coach Jackson and his staff of coaches were implementing. They "got into the wheelbarrow." They became the "original goons," developed and memorized their core values, earned everything (even getting into the varsity locker room), and experienced a season that none of us will ever forget. We went 10-3, 3 rounds deep in the playoffs (further than any team in North Forney's history), and our team impacted the entire community as thousands upon thousands of people attended the games and followed our team into the playoffs.

Never in the program's history had there been that much excitement and belief in North Forney Football. I will always remember the images of all the fans, many with signs, screaming in the stands at AT&T Stadium. Boys became heroes, and men will sit around for the rest of their lives, having conversations about the moments, games, and the incredible transformation that took place that year.

There were bumps in the road. Everything wasn't perfect for sure. Some players quit and not every parent got on board with the changes. There were multiple battles that were fought (still are), but that will always be the case when turning a program around and change the culture. What's most important is that things are changing. We aren't who we were, and it was because a group of players and parents were ready and willing to say "Yes" and a head coach came in and was willing to do what needed to be done to change things.

Throughout the next season, the booster club grew from 5 to 14 officers on the board. Parents and families are already getting excited about another campaign. Even

Culture Defeats Strategy 2 - Goonville, Texas Pop. 11

though the 2018 season didn't have the same results record wise and was filled with unexpected challenges, the culture continues to grow and become stronger, even with the difficulties that were faced. The next group of Goons are in offseason getting ready for next year. Parents are engaging and filling booster club positions, and things are moving forward. I don't even have a son on the team anymore, but I will be at the booster club meeting tonight, ready to say "Yes" again! You see, when you change the culture positively, people don't want to step away immediately, but they want to continue helping build on what they experienced. There is now a legacy that needs to be protected. As any coach reading, this knows, when that happens, you know things have changed!

Coaches, you matter. What you do matters. The wisdom that is in the book on developing a culture in your program can be life-changing. Not just for you, but players and families like us in Goonville. I believe in every community, no matter how big or small, that some parents and families desire to be led. They may not always like, agree with, or understand what you do, but if you lead them with passion, love for their kids, and passion for the game, they will follow you. I know that what happened in 2017 was unique. Change doesn't always happen that fast, but you never know unless you try. I hope you will!

@CoachJacksonTPW #culturematters

Culture Defeats Strategy 2 - Goonville, Texas Pop. 11

Culture Defeats Strategy 2 - Goonville, Texas Pop. 11

Culture Defeats Strategy 2 - Goonville, Texas Pop. 11

THANK YOU

2017 GOONS, TEACHERS, COACHES, ADMINISTRATION, PARENTS AND FALCON FANS EVERYWHERE!!

Culture Defeats Strategy 2 - Goonville, Texas Pop. 11

@CoachJacksonTPW #culturematters

Made in the USA
Columbia, SC
24 February 2020